His Majesty's Bark
Endeavour

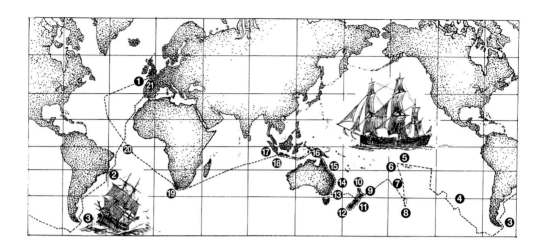

The voyage of HM Bark Endeavour

KEY	DATE	POSITION
	1768	
1	August	Sailed from Plymouth
2	December	Rio de Janiero
	1769	
3	January	Cape Horn
4	March	South Pacific
5	April	Arrived Tahiti
6	June–July	Observed transit of Venus at Tahiti and explored Society Islands
7	August–October	Searched westwards for Great Southern Continent, results negative
8	September	Latitude 40 S
9	October	Arrived New Zealand, Young Nick's Head
10	October –December	Charting North Island, New Zealand
	1770	
11	January	Refit in Queen Charlotte Sound
12	February–April	Charting South Island, New Zealand
13	April	Arrived east coast of Australia
14	May	Botany Bay
15	June	*Endeavour* repaired at Endeavour Reef
16	September	New Guinea
17	October	Batavia
18	December	Sailed for England
	1771	
19	March	Cape Town
20	May	South Atlantic
21	July	Arrived the Downs

His Majesty's Bark Endeavour

The story of the ship and her people

Informative text by
ANTONIA MACARTHUR

Illustrated with
Contemporary paintings, charts and sketches

Line and wash drawings by
DENNIS ADAMS

Angus&Robertson
An imprint of HarperCollins*Publishers*
in association with
Australian National Maritime Museum

Printed in Hong Kong
by Printing Express Ltd.
Printed on 115 gsm Matt Art

Angus&Robertson
An imprint of HarperCollins*Publishers,* Australia

First published in Australia in 1997
Reprinted 1997, 1998
by HarperCollins*Publishers* Pty Limited
ACN 009 913 517
http://www.harpercollins.com.au
A member of the HarperCollins*Publishers* (Australia) Pty Limited Group
Published in association with the Australian National Maritime Museum

The Australian National Maritime Museum has been involved with the
HM Bark *Endeavour* replica project from its outset. The Museum, in
Darling Harbour, Sydney, is the vessel's home port and provides
Membership support and news of the vessel through the Australian
National Maritime Museum Members Program. Tel: 61 (02) 9552 7777.

HarperCollins*Publishers*
25 Ryde Road, Pymble, Sydney, NSW 2073, Australia
31 View Road, Glenfield, Auckland 10, New Zealand
77-85 Fulham Palace Road, London W6 8JB, United Kingdom
Hazelton Lanes, 55 Avenue Road, Suite 2900, Toronto, Ontario M5R 3L2
and 1995 Markham Road, Scarborough, Ontario M1B 5M8, Canada
10 East 53rd Street, New York NY 10032, USA

National Library of Australia Cataloguing-in-Publication data:

Macarthur, Antonia.
His Majesty's bark Endeavour: the story of the ship
and her people.

ISBN 0 207 19180 8.

1. Cook, James. 1728–1779—Journeys. 2. Endeavour (Ship).
3. Pacific Ocean—Discovery and exploration.
I. Australian National Maritime Museum. II. Title.
910. 91

Designed and produced by Maritime Heritage Press Pty Ltd
80A Queen Street, Woollahra NSW 2025
Designer: Lucy Dougherty
Cover painting and internal line and wash drawings by Dennis Adams

9 8 7 6 5 4 3
01 00 99 98

Contents

Foreword

This book sets out the background to the original voyage of HM Bark *Endeavour* 1768-1771. It describes the ship and the men who sailed in her, how they lived, where they slept, what they ate. The excitement of this famous voyage of discovery to new lands and people, plants and animals, is highlighted by extracts from original shipboard journals and logs, and illustrated with charts and paintings made during the voyage.

In the 20th century, to build an accurate replica of an 18th century sailing ship needs accurate research, and one of the first acts of the organising body, the HM Bark *Endeavour* Foundation, was to appoint a researcher to work in conjunction with the National Maritime Museum in Greenwich to do this. Antonia Macarthur was well known as a researcher specialising in replication of historic ships, and respected for her work on HMS *Warrior*, built in 1860. She applied her research skills and tenacity, coupled with a flair for the scent of previously missed details, to support the accurate construction of the *Endeavour* replica.

The result of these years of labour has added a new dimension to the story of the voyage of HM Bark *Endeavour* and Captain James Cook. Antonia's work will be appreciated by all who see the replica of *Endeavour* and I hope that all who read this book will gain as much pleasure from it as I have for it is a worthwhile and accurate reference.

Arthur Weller
Chairman
HM *Bark* Endeavour *Foundation*

Background

On the 25 October 1760, King George II rose early and ate a good breakfast. He then retired to his water closet where he suffered a massive heart attack, and died somewhat ignobly *in situ*. His grandson, George, came to the British throne a shy young man of 22, to rule over a country with primarily an agricultural economy, where the vagaries of the yearly harvest and the price of bread affected the lives of most of the people. The population of England was about five and a half million; over half were under the age of twenty-one and the overall life expectancy was only thirty-five — it was a youthful and energetic nation.

The vast majority of people earned a living from the land as farmers, cottagers and agricultural labourers, or worked at one of the many jobs which serviced the rural community — as thatchers, masons, wheelwrights, blacksmiths, milkmaids, brewers and innkeepers. Most manufacturing industry was small scale and local, often employing whole families, and only a few establishments, such as those in the coal mining and shipbuilding industries, employed large workforces.

Although disadvantaged in law and subject to numerous pregnancies, many women managed and ran large farms and estates with their husbands, or had their own businesses, such as brewing beer, and were often apprenticed to trades such as those of the barber, milliner and wig maker.

There was a wide division between the rich and the poor, and politics and power were both hereditary and based on privilege. As Oliver Goldsmith wrote 'Laws grind the poor, and rich men rule the law'. However between these two extremes was a varied and mixed group of middle class people, who through marriage and business became closely entwined with the upper classes by the end of the 18th century. They included lawyers, architects, teachers, scientists, doctors, farmers, tradesmen, civil servants, army and navy officers and the most powerful group amongst them, the merchants. They had their fingers in many pies: they exported and imported large quantities of goods — woollen cloth and blankets to Europe and America, tea from China, sugar and rum from the West Indies and tobacco from Virginia. The merchants were rich enough to own and control the Bank of England and to lend money to the government — influence and power indeed!

The second half of the century was a time of great contrasts. A mixture of ignorance, cruelty and lawlessness and at the same time of intellectual inquiry, elegance and wit, a hard working and plain speaking society, a lustier and less refined age than the following century was to prove. Although custom and privilege were respected, they were not venerated, and journalists and satirists attacked those in high places and spared few. George III's mother, the Princess Dowager, had to stop visiting the theatre because of the insults shouted at her about her supposed relationship with the Earl of Bute.

Fashionable men and women commonly swore, blood sports such as cock fighting were widely enjoyed by all classes, and members of parliament were known to leave a sitting in the House to bet on a nearby fight. The permanent wooden seats, called 'Mother Proctor's Pews', by the gallows at Tyburn Tree, rarely lacked customers for the frequent public hangings. Crowds pelted pilloried felons with rotten fruit and muck, and cheered when convicted whores were flogged in public, Jew baiting went unpunished and the slave trade continued to make men rich.

Sophisticated society listened to the music of George Frederick Handel and flocked to see Thomas Arne's 'Beggar's Opera'. The wealthy had their portraits painted by Joshua Reynolds or Zoffany and their horses and dogs painted by Stubbs. People of all classes relaxed at county fairs and weekly markets, played bowls, attended race meetings, musical evenings and the theatre; they took trips on the rivers, met and discussed business in coffee houses, gossiped and danced in assembly rooms, took the waters in Bath, and both bathed in, and drank, the seawater at Margate and other seaside resorts. Travel by road became increasingly popular but remained uncomfortable, dirty and often dangerous. Travellers shared their common lodging beds with strangers and bedlice, and highwaymen waited to relieve them of their money and belongings, even in the centre of London.

Local 'societies' up and down the country provided a forum for new ideas. Men of learning, doctors and scientists presented papers and debated a wide range of topics such as agricultural reform, medicine, botany and astronomy. By the 1760s there had been many improvements in scientific and technical knowledge, which were to help solve the problems of navigating ships far from home ports. In 1767, when the Royal Society of London met to organise the viewing and charting of the transit of the planet Venus across the sun, the time was ripe to support a voyage of scientific study and discovery.

This was the voyage that sent His Majesty's Bark *Endeavour* to the South Pacific and on around the world to discover and chart new lands, to study new peoples, plants and animals. It made Captain James Cook and Joseph Banks famous, and became a blueprint for future voyages.

Beginnings

"A proper vessel be prepared"

For centuries astronomers had been searching for answers to the Universe. How did it come into being? How big is it? By the eighteenth century they had some idea of the scale involved, but to advance their knowledge it was essential to work out the distance between the Sun and the Earth. The problem was, how to measure this?

Astronomers knew that at various times Venus passed across the Sun; if the time that this took could be accurately measured, then by using various mathematical equations they could work out the distance between the Sun and the Earth, and this distance could provide the key to measuring the Universe itself!

In 1761, 120 observers from nine countries had viewed the transit, from places as far flung as China, Siberia, India, Turkey, Sweden, Newfoundland, the Cape of Good Hope, St Helena, Rodriguez Island, and a number of sites across Europe and Britain. Unfortunately when all these measurements were collated, the results were disappointing and the need to obtain more accurate figures from the next transit — due on 3 June 1769 — was urgent: Venus would not pass across the Sun again for another 104 years!

The Royal Society in England 'resolved to send astronomers to several parts of the world in order to Obsrve the Transit', and decided on three sites: the North Cape, Fort Churchill in Hudson Bay, and the South Seas

Alexander Dalrymple's chart of the south Pacific Ocean clearly shows the land masses known in 1767. Dalrymple provided Joseph Banks with a copy of this for the Endeavour *voyage.*

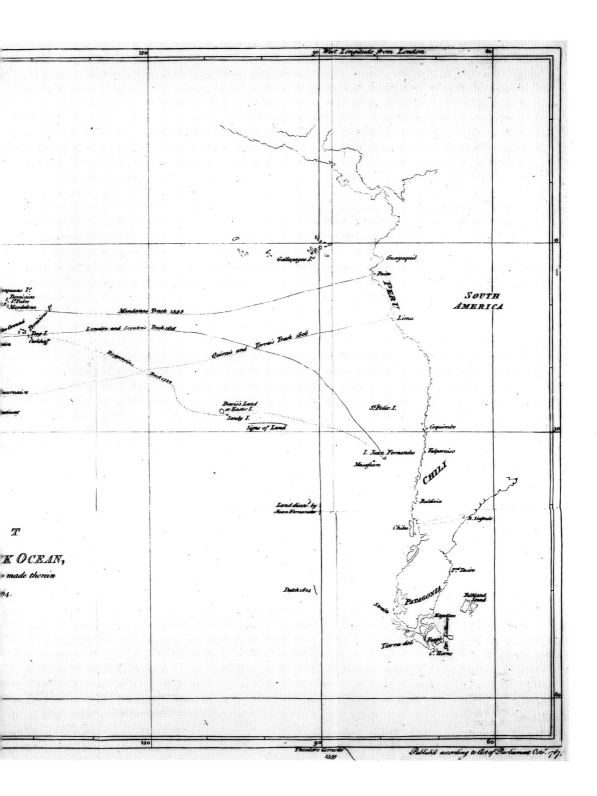

Guayaquil

Paita

PERU

SOUTH
AMERICA

Gallapagos I.ˢ

Lima

Marquesas I.ˢ
Dominica
S.ᵗ Pedro
Magdalena

Magdalene Ground

Mendanas Track 1595

Dog I.

Lemaire and Scouten's Track 1616

Cartshoff

Quiros and Torres Track 1606

Roggewein

Track 1722

Incarnation

Continent

Davis's Land
or Easter I.

Sandy I.

Signs of Land

S.ᵗ Felix I.

Coquimbo

I. Juan Fernandez

Masafuera

Valparaiso

CHILI

Baldivia

Land discoᵈ by
Juan Fernandez

Chiloe

B. Sinfondo

T

ᴷ OCEAN,

 made therein

64.

Dutch 1624

PATAGONIA

P.ᵗ Desire

Falkland
Island

Strait

Magellan

Tierra del

Fuego

C. Horne

Theodore Gerrards
1599

Publish'd according to Act of Parliament Octᵣ 1767.

3

where they hoped to find a suitable island, reliable weather and clear skies.

For many years explorers and writers had talked of an undiscovered southern land which they called *Terra Australis Incognita,* a land somewhere in the southern ocean, peopled by an exotic race, with unusual flora and fauna, and rich in precious metals and spices. One anonymous author professed to have lived in this land, and published a book in 1720 called *A Description of New Athens in Terra Australis incognita.* He gave an account of the 'fortunate shipwreck' that led him to this land, and the delights he experienced from the bad and good women who lived there!

Alexander Dalrymple was a more serious supporter of the idea of a southern continent. Dalrymple had worked for the British East India Company, becoming Deputy Secretary of Madras in 1758, and Deputy Governor of Manila in 1762. During this time he studied and travelled in the seas around Asia. On his return to England, he summarised all the available information about the South Pacific in a 103 page book, and produced a chart of the region between South America and New Holland. This so impressed the Royal Society that it found him 'a proper person to send to the South Seas, having a particular turn for discoveries, and being an able navigator, and well skilled in Observations', and elected him commander of the ship, naming as his fellow observer the astronomer Charles Green.

In February of the next year, with preparations well in hand, the Royal Society presented a memorial to King George III asking for support and funding. The King granted £4,000 'to defray the expense of conveying such persons as it shall be thought proper to send to make the observations to the southward of the Equinoctial Line' and he urged 'that a proper vessel be prepared to sail early this spring'.

Lord Shelburne, Principal Secretary of State, conveyed the King's orders to the Admiralty on 5 March, and four weeks later a Whitby collier called *The Earl of Pembroke* had been purchased for £2,800, registered on the List of the Navy as a bark named *Endeavour* and was in dry dock in Deptford refitting for the voyage.

In the meantime the Admiralty had vetoed the Society's choice of Alexander Dalrymple as commander, it being against naval policy, at the time, for a civilian to command one of His Majesty's ships. Dalrymple would not consider going as principal observer only, and so he withdrew, leaving the way open for a new commander.

Capt. James Cook of the Endeavour.

James Cook was born on 27 October 1728 at Marton, a small village in Yorkshire, the second son of James Cook, a day labourer from Scotland, and his wife Grace. At the age of 18, Cook was apprenticed to John Walker, a well respected Quaker shipowner and coal shipper at Whitby, a port of some 10,000 inhabitants on the Yorkshire coast. As an apprentice, Cook worked long hours with half a day a week shore leave, and for the next nine years he served aboard Whitby colliers, taking coal around the British coast and across the North Sea to Scandinavia. When he was 27, John Walker offered him command of his own ship, however Cook turned this down. There is no certain evidence as to why Cook rejected this offer, but as time was to show, he was a man of action, hard working and ambitious, with a need to sail greater seas. Perhaps a life sailing British coastal waters and the North Sea was too confining and unadventurous a future. Also by mid-1755 the Navy was on a war footing with France, and war offered a chance of prize money and advancement. Whatever his reasons, Cook joined the Royal Navy as a volunteer, at Wapping, London on 17 June 1755, with the rank of able seaman.

A striking painting of Captain James Cook by William Hodges, the artist who travelled with him on the second voyage 1772-75.

With his bounty of £2 and the promise of £1.4s per month, Cook travelled to Portsmouth and on 25 June joined the *Eagle*, a ship of 60 guns. Her captain was Joseph Hamar, who quickly noted the new volunteer's experience and promoted him to master's mate by the end of month. Most of this time on board *Eagle* was spent in the tedious business of blockading the coasts of France.

Whitby Harbour in the 18th century, where the young James Cook lived and worked for his patron John Walker.

Two years later Cook sat and passed his master's exams at Trinity House, Deptford. As Master, he joined the *Solebay*, based at Leith on the Firth of Forth, on routine patrol of the eastern coast of Scotland and the Orkney and Shetland islands, until 27 October 1757 when he entered the *Pembroke*, a new 64 gun ship of the line, under the command of Captain John Simcoe. The war with France had become a trans-Atlantic war, involving British and French colonies in America, and on 22 February 1758, *Pembroke* sailed with the British fleet under the command of Vice-Admiral Boscawen across the Atlantic. *Pembroke* saw very little action until 26 July when she was present at the surrender of Louisburg.

Shortly afterwards Cook had the good fortune to meet Samuel Holland, a military engineer and surveyor, who taught him the art of surveying using a plane table. Holland, who eventually became the Surveyor General of Quebec, left this recollection of their time together:

> *I was on board the* Pembroke *where the great cabin, dedicated to scientific purposes and mostly taken up*

with a drawing table, furnished no room for idlers. Under Capt Simcoe's eye, Mr Cook and myself compiled materials for a Chart of the Gulf and River St Lawrence...

Captain Simcoe recommended Cook

...to make himself competent to the business by learning Spherical Trigonometry, with the practical part of Astronomy, at the same time giving him Leadbitter's works, a great authority on astronomy etc at that period.

After the war ended Cook returned home and was paid off on 8 December 1762. He drew his pay of £291. 19s.3d and hurried to visit a young lady, Elizabeth Batts, who lived in the parish of Barking in east London. Two weeks later James, aged 34, and Elizabeth, 21, walked hand in hand across the meadows to her parish church of St Margaret's, where they were married on 21 December. They returned to live at James's residence across the river in St Paul's, Shadwell.

Four months later Cook again set sail for Newfoundland, as surveyor aboard the *Antelope* under Captain Graves, at a wage of ten shillings a day, a large increase on his previous earnings as master. The next six months

The only known painting of Elizabeth Cook, in her old age. Elizabeth outlived James, her five children and her cousin Isaac Smith, dying at the age of 93. She was buried with her sons James and Hugh beneath the middle aisle of the church of St Andrew the Great, Cambridge.

James and Elizabeth walked across the fields and were married in St Margaret's parish church, on 21 December 1762.

were spent on surveying and drawing, and on 30 October, the Governor of Newfoundland reported to the Admiralty:

> *As Mr Cook whose Pains and attention are beyond my description, can go no farther in surveying this year I send him home in the Tweed…that he may have the more time to finish the difft surveys already taken of it to be layn before their Lordships and to copy the different sketches of the Coasts and Harbours, taken by the ships on the several stations by which their Lordships will perceive how extreamly erroneous the present draughts are…Mr Cook will lay before their Lords the orginal Survey of St Peters Miqueion & Langley as allso Quirpon & Noddy harbours, Chateaux or York harbour & Croque…*

James returned to see his son James for the first time. He and Elizabeth now looked for a new home, something to house their growing family and in keeping with his new position as a surveyor. They bought a small, recently built, end of terrace house, 7 Assembly Row in

Map of Mile End Old Town, Stepney, showing the Cooks' new home at 7 Assembly Row.

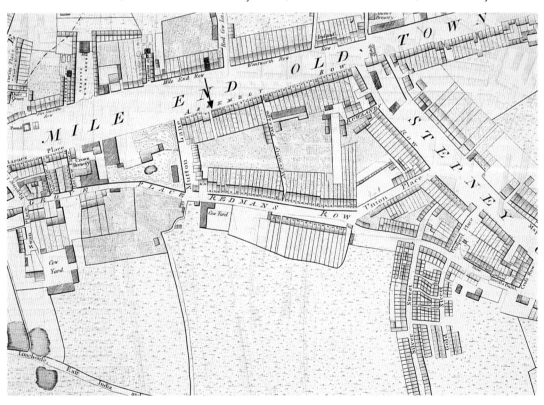

Stepney. It was typical of the small east London houses of the period, consisting of three floors and a basement, with two rooms to a floor. It had a walled garden at the back, and a small front garden which faced on to the Mile End Road, the major road leading eastwards out of London to the coast; people, carts, horses and coaches trundled goods and passengers into and out of the city daily, and the new London Hospital, completed in 1759, was just half a mile away.

Cook's pattern of life continued with summers spent surveying in Newfoundland, and winters working at home on his charts and drawings. During this period he produced a collection of Newfoundland charts that remained the standard Admiralty charts for many years. On returning to England in 1765, he handed a collection of his astronomical observations of an eclipse for analysis, to Dr John Bevis, a physician, astronomer and member of the Royal Society. Dr Bevis gave a brief paper on Cook's eclipse observations to the Royal Society, on 30 April 1767. Now James Cook's name was known to the Society as someone who was competent with astronomical observation, and although we do not know the detailed talks between the Admiralty and the Royal Society when they were looking for a new commander, it is certain that Cook had qualities that recommended him to both.

On 15 April 1768, the Admiralty appointed James Cook to the rank of 1st Lieutenant and gave him command of His Majesty's Bark *Endeavour*. Cook also received a payment of 100 guineas to act as an observer for the Royal Society, with an extra victualling allowance of £120 to be used towards his personal supplies of food and drink.

The *Annual Register* for the year 1768 reported a hot summer with numerous 'tumults and riots' in London. The trouble was over low and reduced wages and there were petitions and mass meetings attended by a large cross section of workers. It was not long before all work stopped on the Thames and the *Endeavour* sat in dry dock in Deptford Yard in the hot sun until 18 May, when she was shifted into the basin, and fitting out resumed.

An important event now occured that decided the *Endeavour's* destination — Captain Samuel Wallis returned from circumnavigating the world aboard the *Dolphin* and reported the discovery of a new island which he had named George's Island in honour of the King. The natives called their land Otaheiti (Tahiti) — and it lay on latitude 17° 30' south, longitude 140° west. Wallis's description portrayed a safe anchorage, friendly natives, abundant food and good weather; the Royal Society and the Admiralty agreed it was the ideal location for viewing the transit in the South Seas.

On Wednesday 25 May, James Cook received the following letter from the Admiralty:

> *Whereas we have appointed you first Lieutenant of His Majesty's Bark the Endeavour now at Deptford, and intend that you shall command her during her present intended Voyage...You are hereby required and directed to use the utmost dispatch in getting her ready for the sea accordingly, and then falling down to Galleons Reach take in her guns and gunners' stores at that place and proceed to the Nore for further orders.*

Two days later Lieutenant James Cook stepped aboard *Endeavour* at Deptford to prepare the ship for a voyage of two or more years.

For the next three months the ship was a hive of activity from early morning until late in the evening. The crew arrived and signed on; each was given a number and entered onto the ship's books for victualling and pay. Issued with a hammock or a swinging cot depending on their rank, they were shown where they would mess, sleep and stow their gear. John Satterley, the carpenter, joined the ship on the same day as Cook, and Lieutenant Zachary Hicks, second in command, joined a week later, on 3 June. Petty officers, midshipmen, servants, carpenter's mates, bosun's mates, able seamen and idlers, the one handed cook John Thompson and the butcher Henry Jeffs all arrived during the month of June. Some were strangers and had to settle in with their new shipmates and quarters, however with a long sea voyage ahead there was no hurry — friendships, likes and dislikes would be forged in time; others had already sailed together and shared the dangers

Seizing with a heaving mallet.

of battles and storms at sea. Three young men arrived having just returned from circumnavigating the world aboard the *Dolphin* — Robert Molyneux, Richard Pickersgill and Francis Wilkinson.

Five seamen who had served with Cook on *Grenville* during the Newfoundland surveys transferred with him to *Endeavour.* They were able seaman Thomas Hardman aged 33 who had sailed with Cook for over a year, and 18 year old Peter Flower who was soon to drown tragically at Rio de Janeiro. William Howson, John Charlton and Isaac Smith were all 16 years old and signed on as Cook's servants. Smith was a cousin to Elizabeth, and was to assist the captain during the voyage with surveying and chart making. Cook gave him the honour of being the first person to step onto Australian soil in Botany Bay.

In July when the Admiralty decided that *Endeavour* could use a third lieutenant, it was another fellow officer from the *Dolphin* who joined them. John Gore, an American, was in his late 30s, and with two trips around the world to his credit, under Captain John Byron (1764-66) and Captain Samuel Wallis (1766-68), he had a great knowledge of the southern seas. Another of the *Dolphin's* crew, Francis Haite, came on board as carpenter's crew. The surgeon William Brougham Munkhouse arrived with his mate William Perry, and his younger brother, midshipman Jonathan Munkhouse.

Letters and orders now passed regularly between Cook and various Admiralty departments. *Endeavour* was to be provided with twelve months supplies and stores, and any additional provisions Cook might request.

It was customary for the Navy Board to issue contracts to local merchants and manufacturers, to supply a variety of goods to Naval yards. At Deptford, Messrs Kemp and Gould supplied extra stone ground glass in case of damage to the windows or stern lantern; bales of red and green kersey cloth came from John Bedford; fishing gear was supplied by Sarah and James Dennis; Mary Eastman sent powder room and storeroom lanterns, and a machine for purifying water arrived from Thomas Sabe. Both the boatswain John Gathrey and the carpenter, John Satterley, received an extra three months' supplies which included quantities of canvas, ropes, casks of nails, lamp black, paint, varnish of pine, tar, grease, brushes, brooms and holystones, lanterns, candles and dozens of other items which they would need to repair and keep the ship in good running order, during the coming months.

On 15 June the Victualling Board issued the *Endeavour* with the following food and drink — 4,000 pieces of salt beef, 6,000 pieces of salt pork and 800 pounds of suet, 120 bushels of wheat, 10 bushels of oatmeal, 187 bushels of pease, 21,226 pounds of bread in bags and 13,440 pounds in butts, with 10,400 pounds of flour in barrels and half barrels for making boiled puddings and bread, 2,500 pounds of raisins, 120 gallons of oil, 1,500 pounds of sugar, 500 gallons of vinegar, 20 bushels of salt, 160 pounds of mustard seeds. To drink there was 1,200 gallons of beer and 1,600 gallons of spirits, together with quantities of tobacco for the men to buy. Surgeon Munkhouse and his mate William Perry saw to the loading and storing of twelve months' medical supplies for 80 men.

In addition to this, the Admiralty, eager to eradicate scurvy, supplied special foods thought to be antiscorbutic, and ordered a trial to be carried out on *Endeavour*. Twenty four pints of a syrup of oranges and lemons, a large quantity of slabs of dried portable soup, 7,860 pounds of sauerkraut and 40 bushels of malt were loaded.

The Sick and Hurt Board invited Surgeon Munkhouse to its offices on 12 July and showed him how to administer the syrup, which was for use in the treatment of the disease, not as a preventative. He was also shown the correct method of preparing the portable soup, which was to be issued regularly with the sauerkraut and malt, and he was instructed to keep a report on their effectiveness.

In the middle of all these activities, the council of the Royal Society wrote to the Admiralty on 9 June, formally requesting that Joseph Banks and his party of seven be allowed to join the voyage. Banks was a wealthy young man of 24 and although largely self-taught, he was already a well respected natural scientist and a member of the Royal Society. In 1767 on returning from his first foreign field collecting trip to Newfoundland, he was excited to hear of the Royal

Society's plan to send a ship to the South Seas, and he had applied early in 1768 to be allowed to join the voyage. He outfitted, at his own expense, a group of natural scientists, artists, field collectors and servants. Space had to be created for eight extra people. Stores were moved, officers shifted cabins, and James Cook was asked to share the great cabin, by rights his private area, with Banks and his party. This great cabin was to become the study centre during the voyage, where Banks and his fellows and Cook and his officers worked, ate, talked and socialised.

Joseph Banks visited the ship many times in the following weeks, sometimes with the entomologist John Christian Fabricius, who provides a glimpse of this busy time — 'in the Spring, as long as the ship remained in the Thames, we visited it frequently to arrange all manner of things for the best, and in the most convenient manner.'

'All manner of things' included some small pieces of furniture, a bureau and a chest of drawers, bedding and clothes, and 20 large chests containing scientific instruments, preserving bottles, a library of books, artists' materials and reams of paper for drawing, drying and storage; also eight tin trunks in which to store the dried plant specimens which they would collect; boxes, barrels and baskets of foods; several casks and kegs of spirits and beer, and items for barter including beads and looking glasses. Two dogs, a spaniel and a greyhound came aboard with Banks's retinue. Space had to be found for them all. At the last minute Banks's friend, the botanist Daniel Carl Solander asked to join, and with his servant and their baggage, was squeezed on board *Endeavour*.

As sailing time approached, quantities of fresh vegetables and seasonal fruit arrived, and a number of animals — a goat to supply milk for the officers and the sick, five or six dozen poultry, some sheep, a pig and a sow with a litter of piglets, together with quantities of their fodder. The poultry were kept in coops stored in the boatswain's boat. Unfortunately some of them and the boat were soon to be washed overboard in the Bay of Biscay. However the sheep and the pigs fared somewhat better being penned at the stern on the weather deck, and the goat, which had previously

Jeremy Manford and the ship's goat during a quiet moment aboard the Endeavour *replica on her maiden voyage, 1994.*

John Bird's 12 inch portable astronomical quadrant thought to be the one taken aboard Endeavour. *It was used to measure the angular distance of the sun from the zenith (the point immediatly overhead), from which the accurate latitude and longitude of the observer could be obtained.*

Sextant

circumnavigated the world aboard *Dolphin* had free run of the decks. As well as Banks's two dogs, there were a number of cats to keep down the ship's uninvited livestock of rats, mice, and cockroaches, and as the voyage progressed the sailors would add pets of their own. As Nicholas Roger says in his book on the eighteenth century navy — a ship combined disciplined efficiency 'with large elements of the playground, the farmyard and the travelling circus'.

For viewing the transit, the Royal Society sent aboard a number of scientific instruments including a transit instrument, a Gregorian reflecting telescope, and a one foot astronomical quadrant made by John Bird. A portable pendulum regulator clock was to be used for time keeping. These were to be housed in a wooden observatory, specially designed by the engineer John Smeaton, and both the Astronomer Royal, Nevil Maskelyn and Cook had a hand in its construction.

The Admiralty also supplied the latest and most up to date navigational equipment including accurate sextants made by John Bird and Jesse Ramsden, together with Maskelyne's new compilation of lunar tables published as the *Nautical Almanac* for 1768 and 1769, which would enable Cook to calculate longitude, the ship's position east or west, by the lunar distance method. Cook was to try out a new steering and bearing compass designed by Dr Gowin Knight and Edward Nairne's marine barometer for meteorological observations. At the time of sailing Cook had the good fortune to have on board the latest improvements in scientific and technical knowledge, as well as an excellent astronomer, Charles Green.

On 21 July the ship with most of her complement aboard went downriver to Galleons Reach, where George Forwood, the gunner, received her guns and a quantity of stores.

Sailing on to the Nore, Cook received his instructions for the voyage. These were marked secret and consisted of two parts, the first covering the passage to Otaheiti and the observations for the transit, together with copies of the *Dolphin's* surveys, charts and drawings. The second part, in a sealed packet, related to the route Cook was to sail to look for Terra Australis Incognita:

You are to proceed to the southward in order to make discovery of the Continent above-mentioned until you arrive in the Latitude of 40 degrees, unless you sooner fall in with it. But not having discover'd it or any Evident signs of it in that Run, you are to proceed in search of it to the Westward between the Latitude of 35 degrees until you discover it, or fall in with the Eastern side of the Land discover'd by Tasman and now called New Zeland.

Charles Green, the astronomer, and his servant John Reynolds came aboard in the Downs, and the ship sailed on to Plymouth arriving on 13 August. An anonymous journal fragment, most probably belonging to the midshipman Jonathan Munkhouse, relates that the following morning 'Captain Cook and I went ashore before breakfast to send an express to Mr Banks acquainting him of our Arrival here. We found the Postmistress extreamly pert'.

Cook took this chart with him. Compiled by Gilles Robert de Vaugondy in 1756 it shows the northern coastline close to the spice islands of Southeast Asia.

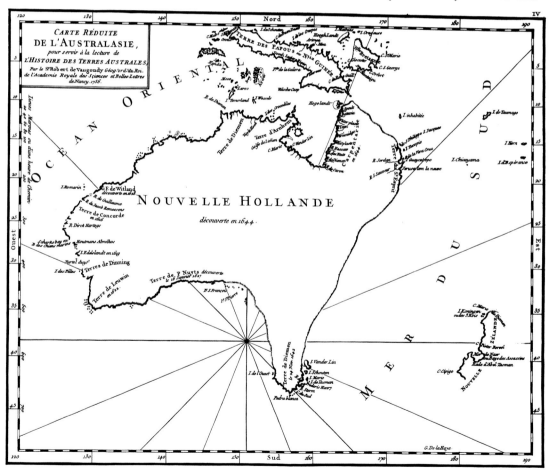

Endeavour *replica under sail during her maiden voyage, May 1994.*

Work continued on board, extra stores of beer, fresh bread and live bullocks were received and the necessary space was found to stow them. The *Endeavour's* vast hold, built to carry large and heavy cargoes of coal, was filling to capacity. The suggestion made by the Navy Board when the Admiralty was looking for a suitable vessel, that a cat-built vessel 'which in their kind are roomy and will afford this advantage of stowing and carrying a large quantity of Provision' would be best-suited, was proving correct.

Carpenters continued to work in the gentlemen's cabins putting up shelves and fittings where needed — and built a platform over the tiller, which gave the gentlemen on board easy access across the quarter deck. During this time the twelve marines joined to complete the crew.

It was a busy time for everyone with many last minute things to do. The Commissioner for the Navy was a welcome sight when he came on board to give the petty officers and the seamen two months' pay in advance; they were able to buy any extras needed for the voyage, either from the purser or from the many small boats stocked with goods and food that rowed out to visit Endeavour. Those who had shore leave could share a last drink and meal with wives, family and friends, and say their final farewells.

Joseph Banks and Dr Solander arrived from London by post chaise, to join the ship. On Friday 19 August Cook recorded in his journal, that the crew 'express'd great chearfullness and readyness to prosecute the Voyage', however adverse winds kept the ship in port, and it was a week later that Cook wrote 'At 2pm got under sail and put to sea having on board 94 persons including Officers Seamen Gentlemen and their servants, near 18 months provisions, 10 Carriage guns 12 Swivels with good store of Ammunition and stores of all kinds.'

On Friday 26 August 1768, Endeavour set sail, bound for the South Pacific.

Taking a sight with the sextant.

The Ship
"No sea can harm her"

Above Deck

When *Endeavour* sailed from Plymouth, although painted in Royal Naval colours of blue, yellow and black, her sides shining with varnish of pine, and flying the Red Ensign, she still looked like what she was — a small and sturdy merchant collier, not at all a King's ship. So much so that Cook had trouble when he arrived in Rio de Janeiro in November. The viceroy, Don Antonio Rolim de Moura viewed the ship with suspicion (were they pirates or British spies?) and he refused permission to land. Gore reported in his journal that:

> one suspicion of us among many Others is that our Ship is a Trading Spy and that Mr Banks and the Doctor are both Supercargoes and Engineers and not naturalists For the Business of such being so very abstruse and unprofitable That they cannot believe Gentlemen would come so Far as Brazil on that Account only.

The English already had a bad reputation in South America for smuggling and the viceroy was taking no chances. He ordered that only the Captain and his boat crew could go ashore and then only under armed guard. Rather than face this indignity Cook refused to go on shore at all and in an attempt to challenge the viceroy's order he sent Lieutenant Zachary Hicks and the boat's crew ashore with instructions to refuse the armed guard. Their boat was confiscated, and Hicks was sent back to the ship under

A VIEW *of the Town of* RIO JANEIRO *from the Anchoring-Place*.

Alexander Buchan, artist, sketched the town of Rio de Janeiro from Endeavour's *deck, during the long hours of confinement on board.*

Bouganvillea collected secretly in Rio de Janeiro, and painted by Sydney Parkinson, artist, December 1768.

guard, while the boat crew was taken into custody, roughly treated and thrown into 'a loathsome dungeon where their companions were chiefly Blacks who were chaind but the Cockswain purchasd a better apartment for seven petacks (about as many shilling English).'

Joseph Banks formally applied for leave to go ashore and was politely refused; however he, Dr Solander and their servants spent many nights ashore as Sydney Parkinson related 'we frequently, unknown to the sentinel stole out of the cabin window at midnight, letting ourselves down into a boat by rope...' They smuggled other plants aboard as Solander reported from Rio by letter to the Earl of Morton, President of the Royal Society 'we have got them on board under the name of Greens For our Table. Now and then have we botanised in the bundles of Grass that have been brought for our Goats and Sheep.'

The viceroy allowed Cook to provision the ship and surgeon Munkhouse went ashore daily, under armed guard, to oversee this, obtaining everything that they needed. Cook sent angry letters to the viceroy, who replied in courteous terms. However, de Moura held to his decision not to allow free access ashore, whatever his real reasons. An already furious Cook was subjected to further insult when, on 5 December, with the pilot on board to take them to sea, *Endeavour* received two shots over her mast from the fort of Santa Cruz. They hove to and Cook sent a boat to inquire the reasons for this, and was told the fort had not received orders to allow them to pass. Banks notes in his journal 'many curses were this day expended on his excellence'. A petty officer was sent to the viceroy and soon returned with a letter to allow them to pass. The letter had been written some days before, but somehow had been 'overlooked'. By this time there was no wind to take them out of harbour, so they waited another two days before *Endeavour* could leave Rio de Janeiro and head south.

When the Admiralty purchased *Endeavour* she was just four years old and the Navy Board referred to her as a 'cat-built bark'. The 18th century naval architect Fredrik af Chapman distinguishes a bark and a cat as two separate classes, the main differences being in the shape of the stern. There has been much academic discussion about a correct definition, and the issue is competently argued and illustrated by David MacGregor in *Merchant Sailing Ships 1775–1815*.

The lines plan and general arrangement drawings taken off during survey, show a long box-like body with a flat bottom, full bilges and vertical sides: her length on the lower deck was 97 feet 8 inches (29.8 m), extreme breadth 29 feet 2 inches (8.9 m). She had five small rectangular loading ports for coal either side, two larger loading ports on the bow and a further two on the stern, for loading long items such as timber and spars. Five extra ports were added during conversion to provide air and light to the new cabins.

Endeavour had three masts and was 'ship rigged' — carrying square sails on each mast. Again there is much

Endeavour's profile and lines plan show a long box-like body and flat bottom, ideal for running ashore for any necessary repairs. This plan was taken during her refit at Deptford in 1768. The blue lines show her decks as the Earl of Pembroke, *and the red lines are the Admiralty additions for the voyage.*

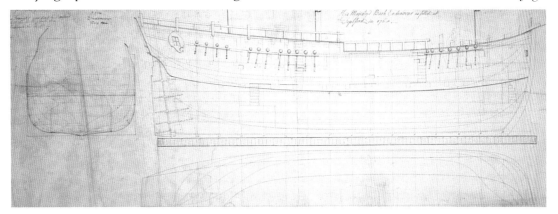

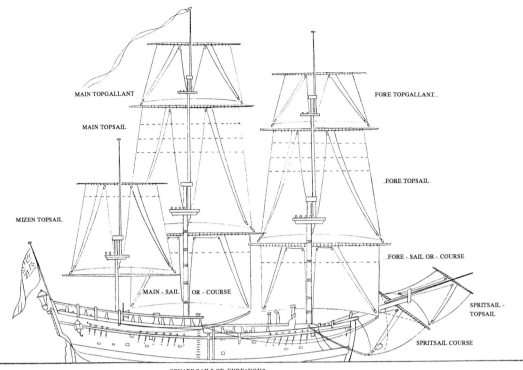

MAIN TOPGALLANT

MAIN TOPSAIL

MIZEN TOPSAIL

MAIN - SAIL   OR - COURSE

FORE TOPGALLANT

FORE TOPSAIL

FORE - SAIL OR - COURSE

SPRITSAIL - TOPSAIL

SPRITSAIL COURSE

SQUARE SAILS OF *ENDEAVOUR*

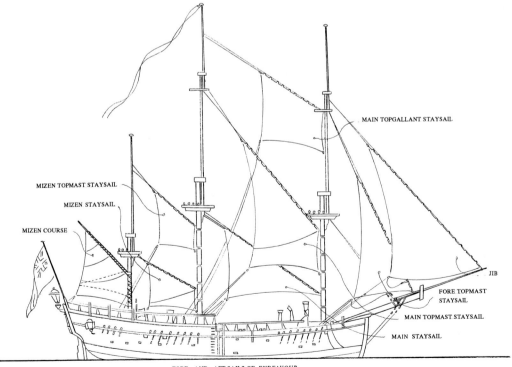

MAIN TOPGALLANT STAYSAIL

MIZEN TOPMAST STAYSAIL

MIZEN STAYSAIL

MIZEN COURSE

JIB

FORE TOPMAST STAYSAIL

MAIN TOPMAST STAYSAIL

MAIN STAYSAIL

FORE - AND - AFT SAILS OF *ENDEAVOUR*

debate over 18th century rigging and sail plans. The full rigging and sail plan decided for the *Endeavour Replica* is illustrated here.

Sails were made of heavy linen canvas, and most of the crew, when not busy, were enlisted to help mend and repair them. This obviously was not always a welcome chore, and when seaman John Thurman refused to assist the sailmaker with repairs, he received a dozen lashes. There were many other uses for canvas on board — hammocks, canvas buckets, awnings, binnacle and boat covers and old canvas was reused many times over.

The sails and the wind were the engines of the ship, and the loss of either could be a disaster. *Endeavour* voyaging around the world was often far from any manufacturing source, and so she carried a full spare set of sail and a quantity of extra canvas. Great care was taken to keep sails in good repair, and those in store were regularly checked for damp.

During *Endeavour's* refit in Deptford Yard, a new internal deck had been added. This ran the full length of the ship, to provide the additional living space needed for her crew, and is marked in red on the plan. The decks marked in blue show her original layout as the *Earl of Pembroke*. The other additions were in the hold, where platforms were built for the magazine (which held the gunpowder and shot), the bread room, fish room, steward's room and storerooms for the captain's stores and slops (clothes).

Endeavour did not carry a figurehead, however the quarter windows were decorated with a carved badge and her stern with other simple carvings. A sketch by Sydney Parkinson, one of the artists on board, gives the best visual evidence of these. The quarter badge windows were fitted with wooden shutters, and four of the stern windows were protected by heavy wooden deadlights (shutters), which were raised and lowered from the quarter deck above and secured to the rail. The large middle window was a dummy which covered the rudder post.

During the voyage Parkinson made three sketches showing the stern of *Endeavour*, none of which shows her name on the transom.

While fitting out in Deptford Yard, *Endeavour's* underwater hull was strengthened and protected, by sheathing with an extra layer of wood. Firstly the hull

Sailmaker at work.

Endeavour *replica sailing through heavy seas in 1995. Parkinson's sketch (inset) of* Endeavour *sailing through a storm at sea in 1769 with her heavy wooden deadlights securely fixed over the stern windows.*

The best view of Endeavour's *stern sketched by Sydney Parkinson, possibly while repairing on the east coast of New Holland, June 1770. This simple drawing shows the stern and quarter windows, four deadlights raised, carvings, and a canvas awning rigged over the quarter deck as protection from the sun.*

was covered with a layer of thick paper rags and coated with a mixture of horsehair and tar, then a new layer of thin planks was close-nailed over, and caulked: caulking was done with oakum, (unravelled old rope) which was forced between the seams and covered with pitch or tar to keep it watertight The whole area was planed to give a smooth surface so as not to hinder the speed of the vessel, and further protected from worm and weed by a coating of white stuff.

White stuff was made from a mixture of train oil (extracted from whales or fish), rosin or turpentine, and brimstone. Although more expensive than other available protective coatings, it was regularly used for ships on foreign voyages where it was considered to give better and longer protection against worm and weed. The worm *teredo* was a great problem especially in warmer seas, as it could eat through timber in a number of weeks leaving no external sign.

After six weeks in the water at Otaheiti, the longboat was leaking badly and when hauled out was found to be riddled with worm 'in a most wonderful manner, every part of her bottom is like a honeycomb and some of the holes $1/8$th of an inch in diameter'. Cook noted that the pinnace which had been painted with white stuff had not been attacked by worm.

The weather deck plans show the quarter deck, main deck and forecastle with their hatches, companions, scuttles and equipment necessary for working the ship. The companion on the quarter deck was framed all round with sash lights (small panes of glass) and fitted with a sash and grating over the top, which gave good light to the officers' wardroom below.

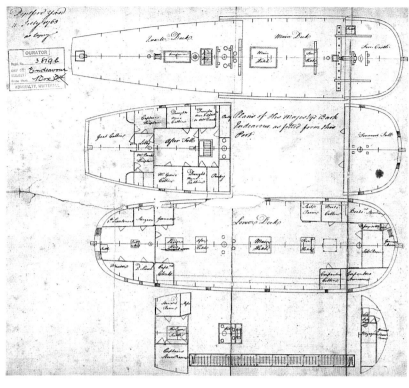

These plans by Deptford Yard in 1768 show the final deck layout, and the new cabins fitted to accommodate Joseph Banks, his party and the officers.

Working the Ship

Steering was done by the rudder, tiller and wheel. A rope was wrapped around the drum of the wheel, and passed through blocks directly below, then to blocks either side of the deck and taken aft through other blocks and secured to the end of the tiller; as the wheel was spun the tiller moved to port or starboard, which in turn moved the rudder to steer the ship. The sweep of the tiller and the ropes made this area of the quarter deck difficult to walk across. A special platform provided a bridge over them for the gentlemen to use and it also housed, above and below, the pens for the sheep and the pigs.

Diagram of steering mechanism.

At the wheel.

Two ship's compasses were set in the binnacle, which was mounted on the deck just ahead of the wheel. The helmsman was given the course to steer and if the wind direction made it possible to lay the course by compass then he did so. However when this was impossible and the ship had to work to windward, then he would steer by wind, watching the action of the wind in the sails and aiming to keep the ship up to the wind as close as possible without slowing her down.

Communications on board were simple. Orders were given with the human voice passed from one officer to another, and assisted when necessary by a speaking trumpet; the ship's bell told the watch, and marine drummer Thomas Rossiter beat everyone to dinner and to quarters. The captain and official visitors were piped aboard by boatswain Gathrey's whistle, and important visitors were sometimes welcomed by a party of marines. When the *Endeavour* arrived at the island of Savu in September 1770, the marines, under Sergeant John Edgcumbe, welcomed the Rajah on board, as he came to have dinner with Cook and Banks. On his departure the Rajah asked to see the marines exercise their arms, which they did and delighted him by firing three rounds in his honour. As the longboat carried them ashore the Rajah and his party 'saluted the ship with three cheers, which the ship answered with five guns'.

It was unlikely that *Endeavour* would be engaged in any serious fighting during her voyage, however she was armed with ten four pounder,

The binnacle.

muzzle loading cannon, and twelve swivel guns, mainly to deter natives and pirates. She encountered no pirates, but the cannon came in handy in the Bay of Islands, New Zealand. Cook and a party were ashore collecting wild celery, when they suddenly found themselves surrounded by a few hundred hostile natives. Lieutenant Zachary Hicks who was in charge on the ship reported that 'suspecting what afterwards fell out', those on the ship 'got a Spring on the Best Bower… we Veerd away and brought her broadside to bear and fired 5 four Pound Shot over them…'

This action scattered the natives and the shore party was left in peace.

The design of *Endeavour's* anchors had changed little since ancient times, and consisted of four parts, the shank, the arms, the stock and the ring. The logs show that she carried at least six anchors, two bowers (the best bower and the small bower were most freqently used and kept ready in the bows), two stream anchors, a coasting anchor and a kedge anchor.

Photograph of Endeavour *replica guns. These were cast from the original 4 pounders that were thrown overboard at Endeavour River…and they can be fired.*

Capstan

The anchors and other heavy items were lifted by two machines, the windlass and the capstan. Both were fitted with removable bars and were simple rotating barrels around which the cables were wound. The windlass's barrel was fixed horizontally and seamen pulled downwards to rotate it; the capstan's barrel was set vertically and seamen braced the bars against their chests, wrapped their arms under and around, and pushed forward. Both the windlass and the capstan had a braking system to prevent them slipping backwards.

Like all wooden ships, *Endeavour* leaked, and water came in from above and below. This water settled in the lowest part of the ship and had to be removed by pumping. There were four lift pumps fitted in a well round the main-mast, and this well extended down through the decks to the lowest level in the ship. The pumps were placed on each side of the keel so the water could be pumped out

Relative size of best bower anchor.

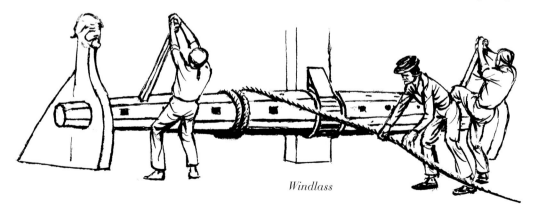

Windlass

regardless of which way the ship was listing. They were never used with more determination than when the ship hit the reef off New South Wales, (the Great Barrier Reef) on 10 June 1770. With one pump broken everyone on board including the naturalists, manned the remaining three for 24 hours, when Banks takes up the story:

> *The most critical part of our distress now aproachd: the ship was almost afloat and every thing ready to get her into deep water but she leakd so fast that with all our pumps we could just keep her free: if (as was probable) she should make more water when hauld off she must sink and we well knew that our boats were not capable of carrying us all ashore the anziety in every bodys countenance was visible enough…At 1 O'clock she floated and was in a few minutes hawld into deep water where to our great satisfaction she made no more water than she had done.*

Then an incorrect reading of the depth of water in the hold was taken and it appeared that the water was gaining on the pumps. Cook reports that for the first time it 'caused fear to operate upon every man in the Ship…they redoubled their Vigour in so much that before 8 o'clock in the Morning they gain'd considerably upon the leak.'

The *Endeavour* carried a longboat and a pinnace both built by Mr Burr at Deptford, also a yawl and a barge, and two small boats, one for the boatswain and one that belonged to Banks. There are numerous references in the journals and logs to their constant use, for the boats were the ship's work horses; they transported officers and crew from ship to shore, enabled visits and messages to be passed between ships at anchor and at sea, ferried supplies, moved ahead of the ship taking soundings in unknown waters, towed the ship in times of calm and were taken on reconnaisance trips in foreign waters.

During days of calm at sea Banks and his servants rowed his small boat around the ship, netting sea creatures and plants, or shooting birds for study and for the pot. On 3 March 1769, becalmed in the Pacific on their way to New Zealand, they shot 69 birds and found a large

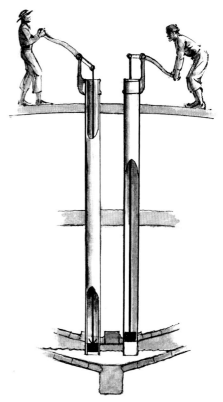

Diagram of lift pumps.

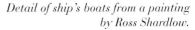

Detail of ship's boats from a painting by Ross Shardlow.

dead floating cuttle fish 'his species could not be determined: only this I know that of him was made one of the best soups I ever eat' wrote Banks.

The ship's boats were usually stowed one inside the other on the boat booms, and the longboat, due to its size and weight, was most probably stored on top of the main hatch.

Endeavour also carried large oars called sweeps which were used on 16 August 1770. After six weeks ashore at Endeavour River, repairing the damage caused by the coral, Cook had just found an opening through the reef, and Endeavour was sailing out to sea, when the wind suddenly dropped and they found themselves being swept back towards the reefs. Immediately Cook ordered two sweeps to be put out of the stern loading ports, in an attempt to pull the ship's head around, until the boats could be got out to tow her away from the

James Cook and Isaac Smith drew this chart of the east coast of New South Wales showing Endeavour's *track and the torturous route through the Labyrinth.*

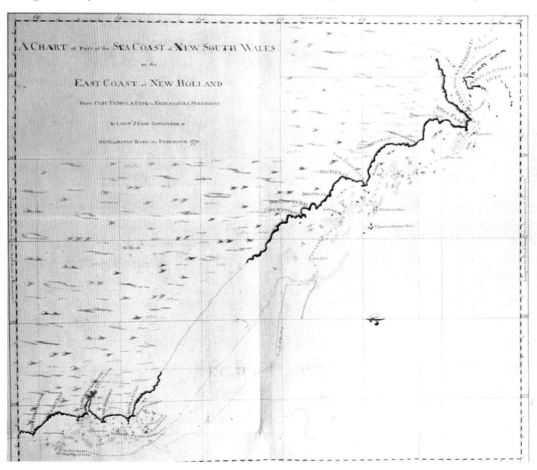

reef. They struggled this way all morning making little headway, when the tide turned and with it came a gentle breeze. It was brief, but enough to allow them to guide *Endeavour* through a narrow opening, and into the calm waters behind the reef. Cook named this opening 'Providential Channell'.

Richard Pickersgill, midshipman, wrote in his journal that it was 'the narrowest Escape we ever had and had it not been for the immeadiate help of Providence we must Inavatably have Perishd'.

Cook then determined to stay within the reef and to search for an opening ahead, and a possible strait between New Holland and New Guinea. He sailed slowly by day, with two boats ahead continually taking soundings, and anchored by night. It was a slow and painstaking course over reefs and shoals, with the constant danger of running aground. Cook expressed it aptly when he wrote the word 'labyrinth' (a maze of tortuous paths) in capitals across his chart of this area. Three days later Cook was out of the labyrinth and *Endeavour* rounded the northernmost part of Australia, and sailed through 'Endeavour Straight' heading for Batavia.

Below Deck

By April 1768 Deptford Yard had submitted to the Admiralty the first set of deck plans for the bark *Endeavour*.

The great cabin at the stern was for the captain's use, as his working and dining area. His bedplace led off on the starboard (right) side, and on the port (left) were two smaller cabins, probably pantries, separated by a lobby. One of Cook's servants may have claimed a little privacy and slung his hammock in one of these. Forward of this were three cabins: one was allocated to Charles Green, the Royal Society's astronomer, the other two were occupied by the Master Robert Molyneux and Second Lieutenant Zachary Hicks. The area between the cabins was the officers' wardroom, where they ate, worked on their journals, logs, and charts, read and relaxed. The glazed quarter deck hatch overhead gave good light and the Captain's clerk, Richard Orton, possibly had a small table or desk to work at. Their servants may have slung their hammocks here at night, to be near at hand when needed.

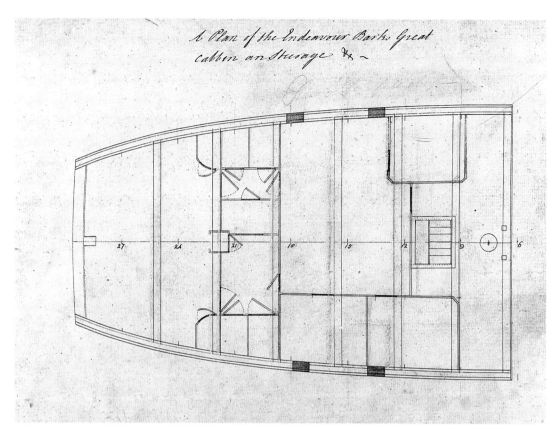

A plan of the great cabin and officer's cabins on Endeavour, *April 16 1768, before Banks and his party were to be accommodated.*

When Deptford Yard was notified that Joseph Banks and his group were to join the ship, new plans were drawn, which show that it was James Cook and his officers who were most affected. Cook lost sole occupancy of the great cabin, which he now had to share with the naturalists. Banks was given the cabin formerly intended for Cook but now somewhat shortened to 6 feet 2 inches (188cm) by 6 feet (183 cm), which he described as 'a place of retirement which just held a Few Books and our papers'. As Banks was 6 feet 4 inches (193cm) tall it is understandable that during the voyage he preferred to sleep in the great cabin. Dr Solander did likewise.

Charles Green remained in his cabin, but the cabin next to his was shortened to make room for the starboard pantry, and two extra cabins were added. All the cabins had lockers built around the side of the ship and each was supplied with a swinging cot if desired. Apart from Banks, they all had a small hatch that was considered high enough above water level to remain unsealed when under sail. In good weather these provided light, air and sometimes the unexpected visitor, as Banks records 'at breakfast another [flying fish] was brought which had flown into Mr Green the Astronomers Cabbin'.

The officers' wardroom was reduced in size, and all the officers now had their cabins on the deck below. These cabins were little more than hutches, approximately 6 feet by 5 feet (183 cm by 152 cm) with a deck height of 4 feet 6 inches (137 cm), with a small hatch and an internal window for ventilation. Although small they provided a degree of privacy, a much sought after privilege on the crowded ship. All cabins were fitted out to Admiralty orders 'to have proper sashes glazed with stone ground glass for lighting the front and to finish the insides with bedplaces and lockers, and all conveniences that shall be required and is customary to do...'.

This flying fish (Dactylopterus volitans) flew into Charles Green's cabin one morning, and was taken to the great cabin to be studied and drawn.

The area between these cabins was probably the mess for the midshipmen and the mates, where they slung their hammocks and ate their meals at a low table, sitting on their sea chests. Although by modern standards this seems an improbable place with its low deck height, again it provided a degree of privacy, privilege and rank. Well into the nineteenth century officers were writing about wardrooms which were certainly no better:

> down still lower to a dark-hole, stinking of pitch, bilge water, cockroaches, mouldy biscuits, damp clothes and tarpaulins...into a pokey kind of den measuring twelve feet long by five feet wide, the entire centre occupied by a table on which is spread a cloth, which may once have been white.

This area on *Endeavour* had two stern loading hatches, which were sealed during voyaging. Consequently there was very little light and fresh air. However when at anchor the hatches could be opened and the wardroom then became a different place, well ventilated and bright.

Forward of the officers' quarters was the main mess deck where the seamen lived: here they ate at tables slung either side of the main hatch and slept in their hammocks.

All meals were prepared on the firehearth, which was a large iron cooking range bolted to the deck. The deck beneath was lined with lead and fitted with stone tiles to prevent scorching from the heat. One end of the firehearth was fitted with a large copper kettle, divided into two sections, for boiling meat and vegetables and making soups. On the opposite side was a fireplace with spits for roasting and two movable arms to hold hanging pots and pans. The fire was laid the full length of the hearth, but moveable iron plates could be slid into place when a smaller fire was required. All smoke and fumes vented through one flue and were released through a chimney on the deck above. There was one small oven for the officers, the gentlemen and the sick. During the voyage, Banks and company ate 'an excellent apple pie' baked from dried American apples. Near the firehearth, the cook John Thompson had a small dresser and lockers to hold his equipment.

Cabins and storerooms on either side of the firehearth were for the carpenter, the boatswain and the sailmaker. In the forward fall the anchor cables and gear were stowed, and below it was another sail room and a passage leading down to the orlop deck below.

Stores and food were kept in large casks in the hold.

This forward orlop platform accommodated the magazine, well below the waterline, where the shot and powder were stored; the aft platform housed the officers' storeroom, the slop store and the steward's room. The steward slept and ate in his cabin, and possibly allowed his assistant to sling his hammock nearby. There were two other store areas below this, which held the ship's bread and biscuits, and the dried and salted fish.

All storerooms were fitted with strong locks, to discourage stealing, and most were lined to keep them dry and safe from mice and rats. Constantine Phipps, a close friend of Banks, reported to the Admiralty in July 1766 while he was the captain of *Diligence*, that all the ship's papers had been eaten by vermin, which were so numerous that it had taken four or five fumigations to destroy them all.

The remainder of the stores and foods were placed in the hold; the traditional method was to stow water in tierces (large casks) at the bottom, set on a bed of clinker (hard bricks or shale), with casks graded by size stored one on top of the other. Each time stores were removed, the ship had to be retrimmed, and when fresh water was pumped out of the tierces salt water was pumped in as ballast.

It was usual naval practice to bring the stores up from the hold onto the orlop deck, where they were weighed, divided up and issued to each mess. As *Endeavour* did not have a full orlop deck, four months' supplies were brought up at a time, and stored where possible on the mess deck, further crowding the 70-odd men who ate, slept and relaxed there.

There is no specific evidence for the interior design and colour scheme of the original *Endeavour*. When a King's ship visited foreign ports, the Captain was expected to entertain local officials on board, and he needed to make a favourable impression as a representative of the Crown. Admiralty orders show *Endeavour* was to be fitted out to many of Cook's requirements, although these would not have extended to any decorative items over and above what was normally supplied. James Cook, in company with other officers of this period, had to pay for anything extra and it was very much up to the captain's individual taste and his pocket, as to how he decorated the great cabin and his own bedplace.

The diarist William Hickey, on passage in the East Indiaman *Plassey* in 1769, wrote that the captain's cabin was 'painted a light pea-green with gold beading'. Another contemporary great cabin was painted in vermillion and green with the columns picked out in blue. However Cook was not a rich man and he had a growing family to support, so it is unlikely that he added any cosmetic touches. It is also unlikely that Joseph Banks, although wealthy, had any such pretentions above practical shelving and storage needs. The money that Banks spent was for equipment, food and drink, and wages for his party of naturalists, artists and servants.

The interior decoration of the *Endeavour* replica has been based on contemporary naval records and 18th century fashion.

The panelling and paintwork are typical for small

vessels of the period. A shipyard specification for a 32 gun frigate built in 1760 requires the interior:

> to be ceiled with slit deal between the beams overhead, both in Great Cabin, Steerage and State room: no pannels to exceed 2'8" [81 cm] in breadth From out to out of the framing, no lining is to be on ship's side and…to have Wainscot Doors to the Cabin and those to the Galleries. To have proper Dead-Lights to the Stern and Gallery Doors with sufficient bolts etc. for securing them, to glaze all such doors and bulkheads and to fit deadlights to great cabin lights and gallery doors etc.

The bulkheads (walls) in the great cabin, Cook's cabin and the officers' wardroom are panelled, the style based on sections of tongue and groove panelling recovered from the wreck of an 18th century merchant ship, believed to be a collier built at Whitby. The remainder of the bulkheads throughout the ship are plain wainscott panels for the gentlemen's cabins and wooden planking for the officer's cabins.

By the middle of the 18th century, fashionable people were changing the colour of their rooms from olive, stone, beige and brown, to newer and brighter colours of blue and green. However sombre shades were still the popular choice for 'masculine' rooms such as studies and libraries, and stone and wood brown have been chosen for the cabins on the *Endeavour* replica. The shipyard specifi-

Great cabin on Endeavour *replica showing the cabin stove, Bank's writing bureau, and the large table where the naturalists and James Cook worked and ate.*

cations show that cabins were painted with 'three coats of priming and one final coat the colour of stone, beige or wood, well ground and laid with linseed oyl'. Eighteenth century stone, wood brown and whitewash colours have been determined by obtaining samples of 18th century paints and matching them by computer to modern equivalents.

Other spaces below decks were either untreated or whitewashed.

Stern windows and carvings. Jenny Scrayan carver, painting the female figures.

Whitewash, also called whiting or Spanish white, was commonly used in houses throughout the 18th century, and was made in two types: that used on ceilings was a mixture of ground chalk and water which gave a grey-white colour and tended to come off as a powder when rubbed; that used on walls was a slurry of ground chalk, water and glue which produced a yellowish white shade, the glue making it a more stable mixture.

The great cabin had four stern windows and two quarter windows, which provided a great deal of natural light and ventilation, making it the ideal study centre for Banks and his group. There is no evidence as to how these stern windows opened and shut, however extant ships models indicate a number of possibilities. The final choice was dictated by the replica herself, for with the two curved top panes of each window fixed into position, the lower sash drops neatly into the stern counter. The sashes are raised by lead weights replicated from the weights found on the *Pandora* wreck. The *Pandora* had been sent by the Admiralty to search for the *Bounty* mutineers, and was returning with 14 of them, when she was wrecked on the Great Barrier Reef in 1791, some miles north of where

Quarter window with carved badge and shutters.

Endeavour grounded. The cabin stove in the great cabin has also been based on the stove from her wreck.

The doors throughout the ship vary in design according to usage — cabin doors are panelled and have small windows, those for storerooms are sliding with vertical bars instead of glass, and the pantry doors have lattice panels for ventilation.

Eighteenth century hinges, handles, hooks and locks were made of iron, as brass was expensive to manufacture and the Admiralty was always frugal. Any officer wanting brass fittings had to pay for them. When Cook was preparing for his second voyage in 1772, now promoted to the rank of Commander, he requested brass door fittings for his cabin, but acknowledged that they would 'be fitted in this manner at my Expence'. There was some standardisation of design and usage of hinges by 1768 and these standard designs have been replicated throughout the ship.

Decks were usually left plain and unsealed, the only coverings supplied being baize cloth or painted floorcloth. Floorcloth was commonly used in houses, and by the middle of the 18th century it had become something of a specialised industry, with manufacturers of cloths handing them on to others to finish with a variety of woodblocked patterns.

A floorcloth was made by stretching canvas onto a frame, sizing with glue and water, and trowling on three thick coats of paint. In between coats, the cloth was rubbed down, often with the leather from old shoes, to take out the lumps and bumps. It was then laid into position, and the design was printed on.

On 30 June 1768, Cook wrote to the Navy Board to ask for green baize floor cloth for the great cabin. His letter is annotated in response with an instruction, to supply baize 'if there is no painted canvas available'. Admiralty documents do not reveal the outcome of Cook's request, however Banks mentions the floor covering in his journal:

> *the floor of the Cabbin in which the experiments were tried, was covered with a red floor cloth of painted Canvas, that had been issued to the ship from his majesties stores at Debtford; which was usually washed with salt water every morning, and sufferd to dry without being ever taken up...*

Nearly 18 months later when they were sailing off the coast of New Zealand, Charles Green, Dr Solander and Banks were testing Green's electricity machine, and Banks reported that 'During all our experiments the floor cloth conductd as it had done before tho it had not been washd for some weeks'— perhaps an insight into the cleanliness and enthusiasm of the servants after two years at sea?

The colour red of the floorcloth posed the same question as the other paints, what shade of red was used? A clue was provided by a fire in 1738.

In March of that year, a paint store in Portsmouth Dockyard burnt down, and the storeman Henry Turner, submitted a list of the paint that had been lost. Two reds were noted, and Venetian red, a brown red shade, was chosen and again matched by computer to modern paints. The replica great cabin floorcloth has been hand sewn and painted using the 18th century method.

The baize floor cloth requested by Cook is not to be confused with the better quality woollen baize cloth used to cover tables and desks. It was really a kersey, a woollen cloth of twill weave, ideal for keeping out the wet and cold, and often used for army uniforms and cheap overcoats.

It is difficult to visualise just how dark the nights were before the invention of electric light. Daily life was regulated by the rising and setting of the sun, and most work was carried out in daylight hours, as Banks noted 'From four or five, when the cabin had lost the odour of food we sat till dark by the great table with our draughtsman opposite…' All lighting on board *Endeavour* was by candle, either in a lantern or candle holder. By the middle of the 18th century there was some degree of specialisation in naval lanterns; hand lanterns were supplied for the boatswain and carpenter, and each also had a triangular bulkhead lantern fitted in his storeroom.

The bulkhead lantern for the powder room was glazed with stone ground glass, and fitted outside the room behind a pane of glass; this allowed the light to shine into the room while keeping the naked flame separate from the gunpowder. For extra safety this lantern was fixed over a cistern filled with water. Fire was a constant danger, and lanterns were extinguished when not in use and always returned to the boatswain's storeroom. They were never allowed to hang alight and uncared for. The firehearth and cabin stove were also extinguished at night and during rough weather.

Boatswain with hand lantern.

Photograph of Joseph Banks's cabin, just enough room for a settle locker, chest of drawers and a few books. The cabin was divided to provide a storage area beside the hull, for his equipment and valuable items. Banks slept in the Great Cabin.

The Navy purchased the cheapest tallow candles for general use. These were made from animal fat, and burned badly, needing constant trimming to ensure a good light. Candles were supplied by the pound, the size determined by the number to the pound, eight, ten and twelve being most common. Matthew Oakes of Portsmouth agreed in 1760, to provide the Navy with:

> *such quantity of tallow candles as shall be demanded for one year…rate of six shillings and two pence three farthings per dozen, of size required…candles shall be white, good sound merchantable, well conditioned, made of English tallow, cotton wicks…I do oblige myself to mark each chest of the candles put therein and not to put two sizes into one chest…and they shall have been made at least two months.*

Cook and the gentlemen probably provided themselves with better quality beeswax candles. Everyone on board quickly learnt his way around, and usually did not bother with lanterns when on the move, proceeding by touch and familiarity, unless working in the hold or one of the stores. An officer or gentleman might light a candle or lantern in his cabin (with the Captain's permission), and a midshipman without a cabin washed and dressed with a candle burning in a bracket in the lid of his sea chest. At lights out, the master-at-arms would check through the ship to make sure all lanterns and candles were extinguished.

James Cook's cabin, the largest personal cabin on board.

The Ship's Company

"expressed great cheerfullness and
readyness to prosecute the voyage"

The Supernumeraries

Ninety four people were aboard *Endeavour* when she set sail from England, and most of them were under 30 years of age. Some were already friends, some were related by birth and some by marriage, some had already served together, and some were not seamen, but supernumeraries, extra to the needs of running the ship.

It was not unusual for a ship to carry supernumeraries, what was unusual about the *Endeavour* was who they were. Astronomers, natural scientists and artists, a group of men who were intelligent, well informed, looking for adventure and eager to observe new lands. One of the most important people amongst them, who was to conduct the observation of the transit of Venus, was the astronomer Charles Green.

Green was 33 years old and like Cook had been born in Yorkshire. He was married to the sister of William

Fort Venus on Otaheiti (Tahiti), built to protect the observatory, and provide living quarters ashore for Banks, his party and some officers and seamen. This pen and ink drawing was done by Charles Praval, a member of the crew taken on board at Batavia in December 1770, and was copied from a lost original by Sporing.

THE WEST ELEVATION of the FORT

Wales, who would sail as astronomer on Cook's second voyage of 1772-75. Many of the officers and seamen had arrangements with the Admiralty to pay all, or part of their wages to their dependents and Green had arranged for half of his wages to be paid to his wife while he was away. Green was an accomplished astronomer and had already been assistant to three astronomers royal, James Bradley, Nathaniel Bliss and Neville Maskelyn.

He was a natural teacher and soon instructed Cook and other *Endeavour* officers in the lunar observation method, as he wrote to the Secretary of the Royal Society from Rio 'I thought it a little odd when I found that no person in the ship could either make an observation of the Moon or Calculate one when made.' Throughout the voyage Green, Cook and his officers Clerke, Munkhouse, Pickersgill and Saunders, and Banks's assistant Sporing regularly discussed and compared their sightings and figures.

When the ship reached Otaheiti the special observation 'fort' was built, and Smeaton's tent with the astronomical equipment was erected. Green now lived ashore and prepared for 3 June, the date of the transit. Cook described this in his report to the Royal Society after they had returned to England:

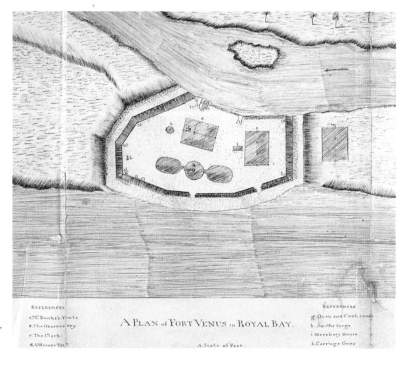

A ground plan of Fort Venus showing the position of the observatory, living and storage areas, and the protective fence: again by Praval from lost original by Sporing.

The astronomical clock, made by Shelton and furnished with a gridiron pendulum, was set up in the middle of one end of a large tent, in a frame of wood made for the purpose at Greenwich, fixed firm and as low in the ground as the door of the clock-case would admit .... The pendulum was adjusted to exactly the same length as it had been at Greenwich. Without the end of the tent facing the clock, and 12 feet from it, stood the observatory, in which were set up the journeyman clock and astronomical quadrant: this last, made by Mr Bird of one foot radius, stood upon the head of a large cask fixed firm in the ground, and well filled with wet heavy sand. A centinel was placed continually over the tent and observatory, with orders to suffer no one to enter — The telescopes made use of in the observations were — Two reflecting ones of two feet focus each, made by the late Mr James Short, one of which was furnished with an object glass micrometer.

A reconstruction of the observatory tent used on the second voyage, and designed by William Bayly. The Endeavour's observatory tent was similar but had wooden rather than canvas walls. The regulator clock make by Shelton (left) and 12 inch astronomical quadrant by Bird (right) were taken by Cook on one or more of his voyages, and the 2 ft focus Gregorian telescope by Watkins (centre) is similar to those he carried.

Dr Daniel Carl Solander FRS, the famous Swedish naturalist was both friend and tutor to Joseph Banks. Painting by Johan Zoffany.

Reflecting telescope.

Saturday, 3 June 1769 was clear and bright, and three parties were formed to observe the transit. Green, Cook and Dr Solander observed from the fort, Lieutenant Hicks, masters' mates Clerke and Pickergill, and Midshipman Saunders took the pinnace to the east and observed from an islet on the reef, while Lieutenant Gore, Surgeon Munkhouse and Mr Sporing rowed the long boat to an island some 10 miles away to the west. The sighting was successfully completed, however final results would have to wait until all observers from around the world had sent their figures to Greenwich.

The natural scientists on board quickly turned the great cabin into a workshop and a meeting place. Here they studied and named plants, dissected fish and birds, analysed, described, drew and painted, compared and annotated; they filled the large glass preserving jars with sea creatures and insects, and stored plants between sheets of paper to dry. Banks took a library of some 115 books on specialised subjects including Linnaeus' *Species plantarum,* Edwards' *A Natural History of Uncommon Birds,* and Dampier's *A Voyage to New Holland in the year 1699.*

Banks gives a glimpse of work in the cabin '*Dr Solander setts at the Cabbin table describing, myself at my Bureau Journalizing, between us hangs a large bunch of sea weed, upon the table lays the wood and barnacles ...*' They worked continuously, stopping only when the sea became too rough.

Daniel Carl Solander was a close friend of Banks. Born in Sweden in 1733, he had been taught by the great Swedish botanist Linnaeus, famous for his system of plant classification, which is still in use today. Solander came to England in 1760 and was employed by the British Museum where he met Joseph Banks and became his tutor. When he joined *Endeavour* he was 35 years old, only five years younger than Cook. A rather plump, good natured man he had a lively interest in people, and like Green he enjoyed sharing his knowledge. Solander's clerk Herman Deitrich Sporing, a fellow Swede, had worked for him for the past two years, and came on board as secretary and assistant to the group.

Sydney Parkinson and Alexander Buchan were artists, talented, young and enthusiastic for adventure. Parkinson was 23 years old and already in Banks's employment as a botanical artist in London. Born in Scotland of a Quaker family, he appears in his portrait an aesthetic, slim young man with dark hair and slender

The artist Sydney Parkinson, thought to be a self portrait.

hands. His output during the voyage was prodigious 'in 14 days one draughtsman has made 94 sketch drawings, so quick a hand has he acquired by use'.

Alexander Buchan's job was to draw figures and landscapes. Unfortunately, and possibly unknown to Banks, Buchan was epileptic. He suffered his first fit during a field collecting trip on Tierra del Fuego, and was left to rest and recover in the care of a servant and a seaman, while the others continued on. The weather in this part of the world can change quickly, and they were all suddenly engulfed in a snow storm. Already separated the party was forced to spend the night out of doors, without proper protection. The next morning Banks's two black servants, Thomas Richmond and George Dorlton were found dead; they had drunk a quantity of rum to

A delicate drawing of a Nephilgenys cruentata *spider by Parkinson; it was then preserved in sand and brought back to England.*

49

Inhabitants of Terra del Fuego in their hut, drawn by Alexander Buchan in January 1769. The basket work objects leaning against the hut on the right and on the roof appear to be drying frames for skins. James Cook said of the huts 'they are neither proof against wind, Hail, rain or snow, a sufficient proof that these People must be a hardy race'.

keep warm and gone to sleep in the snow. Others were suffering from hypothermia and Dr Solander was very ill. Buchan recovered from his seizure on this occasion. However shortly after arriving in Otaheiti he suffered a fatal attack and his body was buried at sea, in case a shore burial might offend native customs.

Two other servants travelled with Banks, James Roberts and Peter Briscoe, who were employed on his Lincolnshire estate. They were both trained to collect in the field, and had already accompanied Banks on trips around England, Scotland and Wales.

At 25 years of age, Joseph Banks owned and managed estates at Revesby Abbey, in Lincolnshire, and had recently purchased a house, 14 New Burlington Street, to give him a London base and house his natural history collections. He was a wealthy young man with a wide ranging interest in new inventions and industry: he travelled around Britain extensively, studying fen drainage and coal mining and adding to his collection of flora, fauna and geological specimens. Banks had spent seven years studying at Oxford University and some months working at the British Museum with Solander as his tutor. In January 1766, he left on his first foreign collecting voyage to Newfoundland and South Labrador, aboard HMS *Niger*.

During this voyage one of those coincidences of history occured, an opportunity for Cook and Banks to meet. On 27 October the *Niger* with Banks aboard, was anchored in St John's harbour, when HMS *Grenville*, under the command of its master, James Cook, entered harbour, returning from surveying the southern coast of Newfoundland. Two days later the *Niger* sailed for home.

Did Banks and Cook meet? It is not recorded. However their lives converged again a year later, as the following letter to Banks from Captain A. Wilkinson shows:

> 'I'd got a Canoe for you which I sent home in the Grenville as she came to Deptford, but she unluckily run on shore and it was wash'd over bord and lost as I am told, tho I have not been able to see Mr. Cook to ask him about it … Mr. Cook lives I am told sme where about Mile end but the Vessel I believe is got up to Deptford that I fancy it will be best to send to enquire on bord her.

By 1767 Cook and Banks had certainly heard about one another.

Some writers argue that Banks was something of a casual student, a wealthy gentleman who joined *Endeavour* with vast quantities of personal luggage, servants at his beck and call and two dogs which he could not bear to leave at home. However this was not the case, and certainly not the opinion of his fellow Royal Society member Dr William Watson, who thought him 'a most expert naturalist, and a very worthy Sensible man.' Banks planned for the *Endeavour* voyage in the greatest detail; his servants were all trained assistants, and his dogs were practical additions to his party — a greyhound to run down game, and a bitch spaniel 'Lady' as a gun dog. In 1764, Captain Byron aboard the *Dolphin* had noted that he wished he had a greyhound or similar hunting dog with him, to catch much needed provisions when they reached various islands.

Joseph Banks painted shortly after his return to England, surrounded by native artefacts from the voyage. Painting by Benjamin West.

Life was regulated by the sounding of the ship's bell.

Shortly after returning from the *Endeavour* voyage, Banks had his portrait painted by Benjamin West. It shows a tall, good looking young man with reddish brown hair, and an intelligent and somewhat sensual face.

The presence of this group of natural scientists and artists had a considerable effect on the officers and crew. On a small ship with little privacy, anything that happened was cause for talk — and everything that was caught, examined, drawn and analysed added an extra dimension to the usual and sometimes boring routine of shipboard life. Before long officers and seamen were bringing fish, birds and insects to the scientists. One week into the voyage, Solander wrote that the sailors

> *soon became such good philosophers that they even recollected the different names and could remember what we had shewn them, and consequently could look out for new ones; some of the sailors have proved very useful to us.*

The crew in turn were eager to share their knowledge — it was an exchange of information both ways, as Joseph Banks noted:

> *Mr Gore tells me that he has seen this weed grow quite to the top of the water in 12 fthom, if so the swelld footstalks are probably the trumpet grass or weed of the Cape of Good Hope...*

Banks and his party lived and worked in close proximity with the officers and men for nearly three years. They shared the discomforts of the ship and the delights of Otaheiti, joined in celebrations, felt the fear, took their turn at the pumps when they struck the reef, and mourned the dead. Their contribution to the general good will and atmosphere on board was considerable.

The Officers

In the 18th century navy, there was not the clear-cut division between officers and men, that became so apparent in the 19th and 20th centuries. Shipboard society overlapped both in rank, profession, age and social class — closely mirroring society ashore.

Officers were divided into two classes, commissioned and warrant. Commissioned officers received a commission from the King and were trained to take command of a ship, while warrant officers received their warrants from the Navy Board and were specialists in their own field.

The most junior of the commissioned officers were the lieutenants. It was quite usual for them to be put in command of smaller vessels, and Lieutenant James Cook was not an exception when he became commander of *Endeavour*. He was addressed as Captain, and assumed all of a captain's many duties. It was a lonely and heavy command, for he had overall responsible for the safety of the ship and everyone aboard. It is difficult in our age of mass communications to truly appreciate this responsibility. Totally isolated from contact with home for most of the voyage, Cook had to rely, in the final analysis, on his own decisions. It was therefore very important for a captain to have experienced supporting officers, and Cook had two of the best. Lieutenants Zachary Hicks and John Gore were next in rank and power to Cook, with responsibility to muster a watch each. In the event of Cook's death, second Lieutenant Hicks would have taken command of *Endeavour*.

Zachary Hicks was born in Stepney, close to where Cook was now living with his family. At 29 years of age he was a reliable and experienced seaman, with the confidence to stand by his opinions. When *Endeavour* was charting New Zealand Hicks' insistance that a strait existed between the South and North Islands proved to be correct.

Next in command, 3rd Lieutenant John Gore, was in his mid-thirties, one of the old men on board. Already having been twice round the world, he was about to make it a third. His feet had hardly touched English soil before he joined *Endeavour*. Possibly the lure of Otaheiti was strong, and certainly his knowledge of the island and his friendships with the people proved valuable to Cook when they arrived there.

Gore was a man with an inquiring mind and great enthusiasms; he had already fought in the Atlantic, the West Indies and the Mediterranean. Now he shot wild duck for the cooking pot with Joseph Banks, took on a native chief in an archery contest in Otaheiti, caught the first stingray in Stingray Bay (later named Botany Bay) and killed the first kangaroo, the strange creatures that many of them had seen, but none had been able to catch. Banks had observed:

> *my greyhound fairly chas'd, but they beat him owing to the length and thickness of the grass which prevented him from running while they at every bound leapd over the tops of it. We observd much to our surprize that instead of Going upon all fours the animal went only upon two legs, making vast bounds ...'*

During the voyage Gore became a close friend of Banks and Dr Solander, and after *Endeavour* returned to England, he accompanied them as a guest, on their field collecting trip to Iceland in 1772.

The most senior of the warrant officers was the Master, Robert Molyneux. His main duty was to navigate the ship, under the direction of the Captain. However he had many other responsibilities. He had to trim the ship — to distribute its weight correctly — and oversee the stowing of ballast, stores and provisions in the hold. He inspected the rigging and sails, compasses, glasses, log and lead lines and was responsible for the safe anchoring of the vessel. Robert Molyneux was only 22 years old, and had just returned from circumnavigating the world aboard *Dolphin*. Like Gore, he probably had just enough time to visit his family in Hale, Lancashire, before he joined *Endeavour* with another shipmate from the *Dolphin*, Richard Pickersgill, who signed on as his mate.

Pickersgill, aged 19, soon proved himself to be a good surveyor and chart maker. He kept an interesting journal in which he made comparative comments with his voyage on *Dolphin*, and good observations of plants and birds. He became a devotee of Cook, and went on to serve as 3rd lieutenant on board *Resolution*, during Cook's second voyage around the world, 1772-75, where one of his juniors assessed him as 'a good officer and astronomer, but liking the Grog.'

The other master's mate was Charles Clerke, a tall young man of 25, with a long nose and a sparkling eye who had also sailed on *Dolphin*, but on the first voyage of 1764. Born

Third Lieutenant John Gore, the sportsman among the officers, painted by John Webber in 1780.

in Essex, he was a talkative and educated man, and had written a book about giants. It is disappointing that such an erudite man wrote only an official journal during the voyage. Like Gore he became a close friend of Banks, and kept up a regular correspondance with him in the following years. Clerke turned down an offer to go on the Iceland trip with Banks, and like Pickersgill joined Cook on *Resolution*, as his second lieutenant. Cook made him commander of *Discovery*, on his third and final voyage, 1776–80.

Midshipmen and masters' mates were defined as inferior officers, which meant that they would eventually become officers. They had to dress and behave as such, and were given the right to walk the quarter deck, the area at the stern of the ship, to which, traditionally, only the Captain and the officers had access. Cook had the right to both promote and demote midshipmen, mates and servants during the voyage, as and when the occasion arose.

All officers were entitled to servants, who to all intents and purposes were apprentices. They cleaned cabins, fetched hot water for washing and shaving, washed clothes, served at table and in turn were trained to their future roles. Servants to the commissioned officers were often young gentlemen under their personal patronage, and sometimes transferred with them from ship to ship. A Captain might have four or five servants, and we know something of Cook's methods of training his:

> *Captain Cook made all us young gentlemen, do the duty aloft the same as the Sailors, learning to hand, and reef the sails, and Steer the Ship, exercise Small Arms etc therby making us good Sailors, as well as good Officers.*

Master's Mate Charles Clerke, a talkative, educated man, painted by Nathaniel Dance 1776.

Three midshipmen signed on at the start of the voyage, Patrick Saunders, John Bootie and Jonathan Munkhouse, the surgeon's younger brother. A general inventory of what a midshipman required on first going to sea gives us an idea of what they may have packed into their seachests: three uniform jackets, a surtout coat and a watch-coat, 3 pairs of white trousers and waistcoats, 3 pairs of nankeen trousers and 3 kerseymere waistcoats. Two round hats with gold loop and cockade, 1 glazed hat, hanger and belt, 18 linen shirts frilled, 12 plain calico shirts, 3 black silk handkerchiefs, 18 pocket cotton ones. 12 pairs of brown cotton stockings, 6 white, 6 worsted, 2 pair of strong shoes and 2 pairs of light shoes.

They took their own linen which included: six towels, and 3 pairs of sheets and pillow-cases. Two table cloths about 3 yards long, a mattress, 3 blankets and a coverlet.

For their personal hygiene: a set of combs and clothes brushes, a set of tooth brushes and tooth powder, a pewter wash hand basin and pewter cup. A set of shoe brushes and a dozen cakes of blacking, or half a dozen bottles. A quadrant and small day and night glass. A silver tablespoon and teaspoon, a knife and fork and a pocket knife and penknife. A log book and journal with paper, pens and ink, and a number of suggested books including Robinson's *Elements of Navigation* and a bible and prayer book.

One wonders if they really took 18 frilled shirts and read these books, or if they preferred one of the popular novels of the day such as Henry Fielding's *The History of the Adventures of Tom Jones*.

Youth is well known for its abundant energy and high spirits, and this found an outlet on board ship — midshipmen and mates were renowned for their rough tricks and games. They had a predilection for cutting down hammocks while people were sleeping or leaving their seachests in the way of unsuspecting officers, especially those they did not like. It was a midshipman who when cheated in a bartering deal with a native in New Zealand, saw it as a just punishment to cast a fishing lead at the man escaping in his canoe, managing to stick the hook into his backside. Tempers sometimes frayed and grievances erupted. Nick Young, who seems to have come on board as an unlisted supernumerary, wrote in large letters across a page of midshipman John Bootie's journal

'Evil communications corrupt good' which Bootie altered to read 'Evil communications corrupt good manners' and added to Nick's signature the words 'is a son of a bitch'.

Midshipmen Patrick Saunders and James Maria Magra landed themselves in a great deal of trouble over an incident with the clerk Richard Orton. Cook described this in his journal:

Some Malicious person or persons in the Ship took the advantage of his [Orton's] being drunk and cut off all the cloaths from off his back, not being satisfied with this they some time after went into his Cabbin and cut off part of both his Ears as he lay asleep in his bed.

Cook considered this assault highly dangerous to discipline on board and an insult to his authority. He wrote

The person whome he [Orton] suspected to have done this was Mr Magra one of the Midshipmen, but this did not appear to me upon inquirey. However as I Know'd Magra had once or twice before this in their drunken frolicks cut of his Cloaths and had been heard to say (as I was told)

Three natives fishing in Queen Charlotte's Sound, New Zealand, January 1770. A pen and wash painting by Parkinson who wrote: 'The manner in which the natives of this bay catch their fish is as follows:- They have a cylindrical net, extended by several hoops at the bottom, and contracted at the top; within the net they stick some pieces of fish, then let it down from the side of the canoe, and the fish, going in to feed, are caught with great ease'.

that if it was not for the Law he would Murder him, these things consider'd induce'd me to think that Magra was not altogether innocent. I therefore, for the present dismiss'd him the quarter deck and suspended him from doing any duty in the Ship.

Cook thought that to some extent Orton might have been partly to blame and adds intriguingly that he himself 'would tend to fix it upon some people in the Ship whome I would fain believe would hardly be guilty of such an action'.

Although he does not mention where his suspicions lay, Cook disrated Patrick Saunders from midshipman to ableseaman and sent him in front of the mast for punishment, but nothing was conclusively proven and no culprits were found. When *Endeavour* reached Batavia, Cook and the officers offered the huge reward of 15 gallons of arrack (a spirit) and 15 guineas, for further information. Saunders deserted, which was taken as evidence of his guilt. Nothing was heard of him again, perhaps he died of fever, or maybe he eventually took a merchant ship back to England. The anxiety of his parents can be imagined, and to be forever on the run is a harsh punishment for what appears to have started as a typical prank, which got out of hand through drunkenness.

Throughout the 18th century alcohol was consumed in large quantities by all age groups. Beer was often brewed at home; it was a thick and nutritional drink and many workers were provided with beer as part of their wages. Heavy drinking was tolerated in the Navy, and as long as a man could turn out for his watch and stay awake, then nothing was said.

When the ship was at anchor it was the job of the midshipman of the watch, to see that all drunken men were put into their hammocks. Drinking was not a crime when kept in the bounds of moderation, and moderation in the 18th century had a wide definition!

The men were issued with 1 gallon of beer a day, and when beer ran out they received 1 pint of wine, or half a pint of rum, brandy or arrack, all of which were watered down. Drink was supposed to be consumed when issued and saving up allowances was discouraged, although extras could be earned by doing private work for officers, who often paid with a glass of spirits. Pilfering was a constant problem and casks were often found to hold less than they should when they were brought up from the spirit room.

It was probably pilfering that led to the death of boatswain's mate, John Reading in August 1769. He died of alcoholic poisoning after drinking three pints of rum. Where he obtained three pints, while the ship was at sea, remained a mystery. Officers took large quantities of drink with them — usually as much as they could afford and had room to store — and a drunken officer was not an unusual sight. In December 1769, a quantity of rum went missing from the spirit cask which stood on the quarter deck, and the leader in this theft was a warrant officer, gunner Stephen Forwood. Cook pronounced him 'from his Drunkenness become the only useless person on board the ship'.

In spite of this, after *Endeavour* returned to England, Cook wrote to the Admiralty Secretary on behalf of Forwood:

> *Mr Forward Gunner of the Endeavour has inform'd me that he hath applied to you, for a removeal out of the said Bark. Permit me to acquaint you that I believe his present ill state of hilth renders him very unfit for such a voyage. I also have to acquaint you that Mr Wilkinson, who my Lords Commissioners of the Admiralty were pleased to keep a gunners warrant Vacant for, is dead, if their Lords Ships would be pleased to appoint Mr Forward to this Vacancy it would give him sufficient time to recover his hilth.*

The Admiralty took heed and Forwood was sent aboard the *Scorpion* as gunner.

Maintenance on board was looked after by the carpenter John Satterley and his mates. They checked to see that the ports were well secured, the decks and sides caulked, masts and yards in good condition and the pumps and ship's boats in working order. Satterley was a qualified and skilled carpenter. Cook said he was 'much Esteem'd by me and every Gentleman on board'.

The survival of the ship could depend on his expertise, and when *Endeavour* struck the reef off New Holland, Satterley worked under the directions of midshipman Jonathan Munkhouse, to fother the ship. This entailed making a bandage from a sail filled with wool and oakum, and spread with the sheep's dung, which was then dragged

The carpenter caulking deck seams.

under the ship and placed over the hole. The water pressure kept it in place until they reached the shore. Once the ship had been run ashore at Endeavour River, Satterley and his crew worked for seven weeks to mend and prepare her for sea. This was often exhausting and frustrating work as Cook explained:

> *At low-water in the PM while the Carpenters were busey in repairing the sheathing and plank under the larboard bow I got people to go under the ships bottom to examine all her larboard side, she only being dry forward but abaft were 9 feet water... The Carpenters continued hard at work under her bottom untill put off by the tide in the eveng, and the morning tide did not ebb out far enough to permit them to work.*

Although they were not able to examine clearly all the damage done by the reef, the repairs carried out enabled the ship to reach the port of Batavia safely.

All 'seamanlike'activities aboard were the general responsibility of the boatswain, John Gathrey, and his mates. As well as handling the ship, they assisted the watch and made sure the men upon deck correctly carried out their duties; they also looked after the rigging, sails, cables, anchors, cordage, boats and associated stores. The sailmaker John Ravenhill was directly responsible to Gathrey and examined the sails before they were bent (put into position) and made sure they were dry before being stored away. Ravenhill was entered on the ship's books as 49 years of age, most likely a necessary lie to get the job rather than a conceit, for Cook says he was about 70 or 80 and 'generally more or less drunk every day'; however he was the only man who did not fall ill when the ship reached Batavia!

While most officers and the marines wore standard uniforms, which they had to purchase at their own cost, there was no uniform issued to the seamen. However seamen had a certain style, and were always recognisable ashore, with their baggy trousers, shirts, jackets, tarred hats and neckerchiefs. Some uniformity did arise during a voyage, as the purser always had a quantity of shirts, trousers and jackets in store, or blue, white or stripped material, and a seaman could buy what he needed. Sometimes he sewed his own trousers and shirt, or paid another seaman to do it for him.

On board *Endeavour*, the Admiralty provided the crew with trousers and jackets of special thick woollen cloth called fearnought to keep out the cold and wet. On 6 January 1769, as *Endeavour* was approaching Cape Horn, every seaman was issued with a pair of trousers and jacket, while the officers received trousers only as they had to wear their uniform jackets at all times. Stocks on board were obviously low by the time they had reached the Cape of Good Hope in 1771, and Cook ordered the following slops (clothes) on 8 April —100 pairs of shoes at 5 shillings a pair, 60 frocks (jackets) and 60 pairs of trousers at 3 shillings 5 pence each.

The Men

Below the officers were the rest of the crew, collectively referred to as the men or the people. Like the officers they were divided by rank and job.

Broadly, there were those who stood watches both during the day and the night, and were responsible for sailing the ship; and those who slept during the night and worked during the day to maintain the ship and look after the crew.

Endeavour beached for repairs on the east coast of New Holland where the ship was unloaded and tents set up on shore, July 1770. An engraving by Will Byrne, from a lost drawing by Sydney Parkinson.

The weather deck of the Endeavour *replica is as busy at sea as the original.*

There was another important group on board — the marines. It was their duty to keep order on the ship and they were also expected to fight to protect the officers and crew on land if necessary. Traditionally the marines lived somewhat apart from the men, messing together and slinging their hammocks between those of the officers and the men, in case of mutiny. A marine was usually posted outside the captain's cabin, and also outside the powder room. When not on duty they wore ordinary clothes, instead of their bright red jackets, and worked at various jobs alongside the sailors, although they could refuse to go aloft.

When a seaman first arrived on board, the first lieutenant gave him a rating depending on his experience: with no experience a sailor became a landsman on a wage of 18 shillings each lunar month, with some experience an ordinary seaman on 19 shillings and with experience to bend and reef the sails and take his turn at the helm, he was rated able seaman and earned 24 shillings. He was then given a number and entered onto the muster books, with his age, place of birth and rating. The muster books kept a record of the days he worked, money he spent with the purser for tobacco, clothes or bedding, and his date of discharge dead or alive. Every man had 1 shilling 6 pence deducted monthly from his wages. Sixpence of this went to the support of the seamen's hospital at Greenwich, and a shilling to Chatham Chest (a fund for distressed seamen). This left a yearly net wage for an able seaman of £14.12s.6d, a good wage compared to his contemporary on land. A 'servant in husbandry' in the 1770s for example—usually a young unmarried worker who 'lived in'with a farmer and received his food— was paid only between £3 and £4 per year.

We know very little about the sailors on board *Endeavour*. Most of them were under 30, some left their mark by being punished, some by promotion, others by deserting or by dying. All but one of them managed to keep Cook's rule regarding their behaviour towards the natives on Otaheiti, 'To endeavour by every fair means to cultivate a friendship with the Natives and to treat them with all imagin-able humanity.' The only man punished was the butcher, Henry Jeffs, who received twelve lashes for threatening to cut the throat of one of the women.

By the second week of July 1769, Cook was ready to leave Otaheiti. He had charted the island

The tree on One Tree Hill, Otaheiti, showing Endeavour *at anchor and Fort Venus across the bay. A pen and ink wash drawing by Sydney Parkinson, April-July 1769.*

and successfully completed the observations of the transit of Venus, and was ready to undertake his 'secret' orders, to sail westward in search of *Terra Australis Incognita.*

On the morning of the 14th it was discovered that two marine privates, Clement Webb and Sam Gibson had deserted to the hills with their 'wives'. Why, we can only guess. They were young and possibly

in love, perhaps they had no family back home; whatever their reasons they held them strongly, for they knew they were committing a serious crime.

Cook could not allow this to happen, but before he sent a search party for them, he reported he was 'willing to wait one day to see if they would return before I took any steps to find them.' Next day midshipman Jonathan Munkhouse, with corporal of marines John Truslove, and a number of sailors set out to search for the deserters. Webb and Gibson were caught and confined in chains on board. Once *Endeavour* was at sea they received their punishment — 24 lashes with the cat o'nine tails, double the usual punishment. It appears that Cook understood their motives, and he certainly did not hold it against them, since he promoted Gibson to Corporal on 26 January 1771, on the death of John Truslove. Gibson continued serving under Cook, as corporal of marines aboard *Resolution* on the second voyage, and as sergeant of marines on *Resolution* during the third voyage, returning each time to Otaheiti! And to his 'wife'?

Life aboard an 18th century sailing ship was uncomfortable and often harsh. However few captains ruled by the lash. Cook punished only 21 of the crew during the three year voyage, one of them John Reading the boatswain's mate for not doing his duty when punishing others — in other words he was too gentle with the cat o'nine tails! Twenty four punishments were given altogether and, apart from Gibson and Webb, only Archibald Wolf received more than 12 lashes — for taking a large number of spike nails from the ship's stores. The primary cause for punishment was neglect of duty and disobedience, usually through drink, and any disagreements that may have occured amongst the men were not reflected in the punishment list.

There was also time for relaxation, fun and laughter, especially when the ship caught the steady trade winds and the sails more or less looked after themselves. Then the men were put to work cleaning the ship, holystoning (scrubbing) the decks, painting, and exercising and drilling with rifles; they were issued with hooks and lines, and fished from the ship, carved in wood, sewed and repaired their clothes, and built model boats.

Sunday, after divine service, was a day of rest when possible, and holidays such as Christmas Day and King

Thespesia populnea *collected on Otaheiti, a plant unknown in Europe. Watercolour by Parkinson.*

George's birthday on 4 June, were celebrated with extra food and drink, music, singing and dancing. There was usually someone on board who could play a musical instrument. During his earlier voyage to Newfoundland, Banks had written to his sister Sarah Sophia:

I have learnt to Play upon a new Instrument as I have Forswore the Flute I have tried my hand upon strings What do you think it is now not a fiddle I can assure but a Poor innocent Guittar which Layh in the Cabbin on which can play Lady Coventries minuet and in Infancy etc...

and he brought his guitar with him on *Endeavour.*

Sailors played a number of traditional games. 'Storming King Arthur's Castle' entailed one group of 'castle owners' repelling another group of 'attackers', and ducking games, which involved a great deal of water, were popular in warm weather. When astronomer Charles Green was returning as a passenger aboard the *New Elizabeth* in 1763 he wrote:

After Dinner we had a general Game of Romps when every one was so Sluced with Water that they might as well have been Duck, except the Captain who was kept Prisoner in the Fore Top. However he fulfild Dean Swift's Prophecy for he Piss'd on Longitude who attemp'd to follow him.

One of the most important ceremonies carried out on the voyage, was one that is still played to this day— the ceremony of crossing the line. Banks described this in detail when *Endeavour* reached the equator on 26 October 1768:

About dinner time a list was brought into the cabbin containing the names of every body and thing aboard the ship, in which the dogs and catts were not forgot...everybody was then calld upon the quarter deck and examind by one of the lieutenants who had crossd, he markd every name either to be duckd or let off according as their qualifications directed. Captain Cooke and Doctor Solander were on the Black list, as were my self my servants and doggs, which I was oblig'd to compound for by giving the Duckers a certain quantity of Brandy for which they willingly excusd us the ceremony.

Those to be ducked were tied securely onto a wooden seat, which was raised high up to the main yard and on

Singing and dancing made for a happy ship.

the boatswain's whistle dropped into the sea. They were ducked three times each and the duckings lasted until almost night. Banks added everyone was amused by:

> the different faces that were made on this occasion, some grinning and exulting in their hardiness whilst others were almost suffocated...

Captain Cook also bought his freedom with drink, as could any of the crew with four days' allowance of rum — however most preferred a dunking.

Cook paid special attention to his own health and hygiene, and that of his crew; he introduced a three watch system, which enabled everyone to get a stretch of uninterrupted sleep and rest, and he encouraged regular exercise and frequent free time ashore. Gore reported when they arrived in Otaheiti the 'Ships co given leave to walk about, as many as could be spared and charged not to injure any native on any pretence whatsoever'.

Cook took regular cold salt water baths, and encouraged the men to do likewise, but it is not known how often they did so. In England, public baths were frequented by all but the very poor, and sea bathing was popular at resorts. But considering the cost and difficulty of heating quantities of water at home and the inclemency of the British weather, it is fair to assume that most people did not bath at home, although many of them washed regularly. On Otaheiti the natives washed three times a day; perhaps in the heat and the relaxed atmosphere of the islands some of the seamen followed suit! One of the things that the modern use of cheap hot water, soap and deodorants has eliminated, is the human smell, or as Banks called it 'the odoriferous perfume of toes and armpits so frequent in Europe'.

All officers and men were required to shave, as facial hair was not allowed in the Navy at this time, and it was common in England to visit a barber regularly if one did not have a servant to attend to this chore. The officers and gentlemen had their own basins and toiletries, and one of the sailors was usually made barber, and shaved and cut the men's hair when required on deck. Seamen usually wore their hair long, tied back in a pigtail which they would sometimes coat with tar, while officers and gentlemen wore wigs. To make these more comfortable men would often have their heads shaved. Some wore their own hair dressed in fashionable styles, bobbed, curled or tied back with a ribbon.

Endeavour was fitted with two wooden seats of ease, lavatories, over the bow, at the front of the ship; sailors sat on these facing forward, with just the wind and sea below. Two seats were obviously not sufficient for all the crew, and it is probable that buckets were also supplied to be used on deck, and emptied overboard when finished. Some ships at this time, were fitted with a urinal called a 'pissdale' on the weather deck, with a lead pipe to take the effluent away over the side. Another favoured place was in the chains, part of the standing rigging which held the masts in place. Here a sailor tied himself on, pointed to the sea and prayed the ship did not heel over and half drown him. Those with cabins had their own night stools or chamber pots, which their servants would empty and clean — after all it was the 18th century and little privacy was needed or worried about either on board or on land. A French visitor to England in 1784, Monsieur la Rochefoucauld, wrote home about a surprising English habit that took place at the dining table after the ladies had left the room, and the men had got down to the serious business of talking, smoking and drinking:

Seats of ease where the seamen sat facing forward with just wind and sea below.

> *The side board is furnished with a number of chamber pots and it is common practice to relieve oneself whilst the rest are drinking: one has no kind of concealment.*

On *Endeavour* the officers and crew performed likewise.

The question of cleaning after using the seats of ease remains debatable. Paper was an expensive commodity, and on land various substances were available, linen towels, wooden scrapers and leaves. It is most probable that a combination of hand, cloth and water was used on board.

After receiving his number and hammock, each sailor was allocated a place to sleep which depended on his

Replica 1760 chamber pots for the officers' use. They are modelled on extant pots at the Wellcome Institute of Medicine, London.

rank and job. He slung his hammock in a space just 14 inches wide, and slept, ate and lived with most of his shipmates on the mess deck. It was a crowded and noisy place, and with the hatches battened down, and the firehearth alight to cook the ship's food, it must have been 'snug' indeed.

Officers were allowed slightly more space, 18 inches, to sling their double hammocks. These were similar to ordinary hammocks, but had two clews, instead of one, at each end, to keep them open. The gentlemen and officers on *Endeavour* were issued with swinging cots, which Falconer describes in his *Marine Dictionary* of 1769 as:

> *A particular sort of bed-frame, suspended from the beams of a ship, for the officers to sleep in between the decks. This contrivance is much more convenient at sea than either the hammocks or fixed cabins, being a large piece of canvas sewed into the form of a chest, about six feet long, one foot deep, and from two to three feet wide: it is extended by a square wooden frame with a canvas bottom, equal to its length and breadth, to retain it in an horizontal position.*

Everyone brought his own bedding with him, or bought it from the purser, who then charged the costs against his wages — on *Endeavour* the bedding cost 10 shillings 6 pence. Bedding usually comprised a mattress, pillow, blankets and coverlet. In 1765, a London slopseller Charles James, was contracted to supply the Navy with bedding to the following standard: mattresses 5 feet 10 inches by 2 feet 1 inch and bolsters 1 foot 9 inches by 1 foot 2 inches, both made from good Bremin (woollen) cloths and stuffed with good clean sweet wool and white or grey flocks. The mattress had to have 12 tacks and together with the bolster was to weigh 10 pounds and cost 5 shillings 4 pence. The Yorkshire woollen blankets and coverlets cost 2 shillings 4 pence each. Based on these figures, the purser on *Endeavour* would have made a profit of 6 pence per bed.

Most of a seaman's life was prescribed; he was told where to sleep, what his job was, and the hours he would work; however one thing he could decide for himself, was who he messed (ate) with. On *Endeavour* six seamen messed together, and each owned a wooden bowl, a wooden or pewter mug, a spoon and a knife. All these items, apart from his knife which he kept with him at all times, were

Swinging the lead to find the depth.

stored in mess shelves above the table. Seamen sat on wooden chests provided by the Navy, in which they kept their belongings, usually sharing one chest between three or four. With such limited space, they brought few things with them, a change of clothes, perhaps a good jacket to wear ashore, a mattress, pillow and blankets for their hammocks, a keepsake from a loved one, a book if they could read, and maybe a favourite pipe if they smoked. Any valuables they gave to the first Lieutenant for safe keeping. Tobacco could be bought once a month from the steward, who weighed it out on deck and issued tobacco and pipes on the forecastle, and here the men relaxed, talked and smoked. As smoking was allowed only at certain times, and never below decks, many sailors chewed tobacco.

Compared to the labouring classes on land, the seamen ate well, if at times somewhat monotonously. John Thompson and his mates cooked and served a hot dinner every day, with meat four days a week and cheese the other three, and bread and beer. Fresh fish, vegetables and fruit were added whenever available.

As *Endeavour* was on a foreign voyage, oil was substituted for most of the butter, and they carried flour, wheat, oatmeal, suet, raisins, vinegar, stockfish (dried cod), and portable soup which was made from dried beef

On the mess deck over 70 men slept, ate and relaxed.

STANDARD WEEKLY RATION PER MAN								
	Bread	Beer	Beef	Pork	Pease	Oatmeal	Butter	Cheese
Sunday	1 lb	1 gal	-	1 lb	½ pint	-	-	-
Monday	1 lb	1 gal	-	-	-	1 pint	2 oz	4 oz
Tuesday	1 lb	1 gal	2 lbs	-	-	-	-	-
Wednesday	1 lb	1 gal	-	-	½ pint	1 pint	2 oz	4 oz
Thursday	1 lb	1 gal	-	1 lb	½ pint	-	-	-
Friday	1 lb	1 gal	-	-	½ pint	1 pint	2 oz	4 oz
Saturday	1 lb	1 gal	2 lbs	-	-	-	-	-

stock. Sauerkraut and malt were additional as a prevention against scurvy.

All cooking was done on the firehearth and the majority of the seamen's meals were boiled in the large copper kettles. Breakfast was usually a type of porridge, a mixture of wheat, vegetables and portable soup, liked by the men and so good that all the officers and the gentlemen also ate it.

Dinner, the main meal of the day was served at 12 noon, when it was traditional for everyone who could be spared, to dine together. Not only was this practical, considering the difficulty of cooking and serving with limited space and implements, but it also created a time to socialise and relax as a group, and was interrupted only by war or bad weather.

Each mess elected its own mess cook, who collected the uncooked food from the steward, placed it in a net bag, and took it to the firehearth. Here the cook marked it with a wooden tally, and placed the bag in the large kettles of water to boil. When ready, the mess cook collected his bag in a wooden bucket and served it to his messmates.

It was in the Navy's interest to keep its seamen healthy, and all captains were instructed to provide fresh food as often as possible. The problem was how to keep food fresh during long sea voyages. Salted meat and dried fish were successfuly stored for many months, but fresh fruits and vegetables, especially greens, were impossible to keep for any length of time. There was limited space to keep livestock for all the crew and the larger animals, such as oxen, often died quickly from the cold and stress. Before cooking, the highly salted beef and pork was first soaked in fresh water in a tub, or towed overboard to help remove the salt. The meat was then boiled with any available vegetables such as onions, potatoes and pumpkins.

On *Endeavour* sauerkraut was served daily, to be eaten as a preventative against scurvy. Rather than order the men to eat this, Cook let it be known that it was for the officers, but the men could have sauerkraut if they wished…his psychology worked so well, that it eventually had to be rationed! Whenever they reached land, Cook led by example, and collected fresh greens for cooking and for salads. He sent shore parties to collect wild celery, scurvy grass and a variety of unknown plants, which Banks and Solander helped identify for the cooking pot.

The iron firehearth where all meals were cooked.

It has often been said that seamen were extremely conservative eaters; however, although the importance of vitamins was not understood, it was common knowledge to all seamen that by eating fresh foods they did not get scurvy, and the *Endeavour* journals show that everyone ate a wide variety of fresh foods whenever available. Robert Molyneux, the Master, reported that on Otaheiti the men ate large amounts of coconuts, plantains, bananas, breadfruit, apples, yams and other roots and fruits, together with fresh meat and fish. Wild celery was gathered in New Zealand and cooked with pease. Lieutenant Gore with Joseph Banks and his dogs hunted birds for the pot; in Botany Bay, Charles Green reported that they caught great quantities of fish, and served 5 pounds to each man. So much fish was left over that it was salted for future eating by individual messes. While they were on the New South Wales coast repairing the ship, kangaroo, turtle, skeat and giant clams were cooked and shared amongst them; hooks and lines were regularly issued to the crew, and boats were sent out daily with fishing nets, and a man from each mess helped with the hauling.

Cook stated his policy regarding food during this time:

Whatever refreshment we got that would bear a division I caused to be equally divided amongest the whole compney generally by weight, the meanest person in the Ship had an equal share with myself or any one on board, and this method every commander of a Ship on such a Voyage as this ought ever to observe.

The captain and the officers were allowed the same food as the men, and they usually brought extra supplies with them. They were allowed to keep live sheep, pigs and poultry for meat and eggs, and goats for milk. Their servants prepared and cooked their meals, roasting, frying and grilling on the open firehearth, and baking in the oven. Banks noted a recipe for cooking albatross, which needed to be skinned and soaked overnight in salt water 'then parboil them and throw away the water, then stew them well with very little water and when sufficiently tender serve them up with Savoury sauce.'

They all ate widely of a variety of animals, birds and fish, even native dogs and rats. Robert Molyneux commented on the good eating that the very fat and tame rats on Otaheiti made.

Later Captain William Bligh (of *Bounty* fame), made an interesting comment which shows the effects of the introduction of alien animals on native fauna...

When I was at Otaheiti with Captain Cook there were great numbers of rats about all the houses, and so tame ...but at this time [on Bounty *1789], we scarce ever saw a rat, which must be attributed to the industry of a breed of cats left here by European ships.*

Bligh had been master on the *Resolution*, during Cook's third voyage around the world, 1776-1780.

The ship's water supply was stored in large wooden casks, and over a period of time it often became foul tasting and rank. In March 1769, Banks mentions that the water taken aboard at Tierra del Fuego three months earlier, was still clear and fresh, which the seamen told him was very rare. Whenever *Endeavour* reached land, Cook sent watering parties ashore, to locate fresh water supplies and refill the casks.

At sea, men suffered from a variety of common complaints, ruptures from hauling on heavy ropes, agues and rheumatism from damp conditions, ulcers and scurvy, which was the greatest single cause of death at sea. Scurvy is caused by a lack of ascorbic acid, or vitamin C, which is essential for the correct function of all cells in the body. The disease results in fatigue and depression, followed by haemorrhages, swollen joints and split gums and skin. If untreated it leads to death. Melancholia (depression and mental illness) was well recognised, due to being confined in a small ship with little variation in work or companions, for months at a time.

Ships' surgeons were not usually well liked, an understandable sentiment considering that many treatments were painful and unhelpful. A surgeon had to provide his own medical instruments, and the Admiralty provided a chest of medicines, which was surveyed by the Physician of Greenwich Hospital, and locked and sealed before it came on board. The surgeon not only had to treat the sick and injured, he was also responsible for obtaining extra food for them wherever possible. William Brougham Munkhouse, *Endeavour's* surgeon, ordered sago and almonds before they left England, and purchased fresh

A rare sketch by James Cook showing the Endeavour *crew filling casks with fresh water in Tolaga Bay, New Zealand, January 1770.*

foods in Rio. When they were repairing the ship after hitting the reef, he regularly rowed up the Endeavour River, to collect fresh greens and fruit, palm cabbage, wild beans and purslane for his patients.

If a sick bay was required at sea, a small area was canvased off between decks, and when they reached land a special tent for the sick was set up ashore. Hygiene below decks was also Munkhouse's duty. Cook was strict about cleanliness and made sure the decks, storerooms and lockers were washed down regularly. A mixture of brimstone and vinegar was burnt to fumigate and kill the cockroaches and lice, while traps and the cats kept the rats and mice down to acceptable levels. Numerous flies, probably accompanying the chickens, sheep and pigs, were a nuisance, but provided food for a yellow wagtail that Banks kept in the great cabin. Unfortunately it was not long before the wagtail, in turn, provided food for one of the ship's cats.

All bedding was aired regularly, and clothes and hammocks were washed when the weather permitted, and hung on the ships rigging to dry. Clothes were often put in a bag or tied to a rope and towed behind the ship to clean them, and sometimes they entangled the odd crab or sea creature for Solander or Banks to study. The gentlemen lost the occassional linen shirt and trousers to curious natives investigating the laundry bag.

A ship's surgeon was required to keep a day book of illness and treatments, and to write two journals from this, one on his physical practice and the other on any surgical operations he performed. These had to be delivered to the physicians in the Commission of Sick and Wounded, or to the Physician of Greenwich Hospital, at the end of the voyage. It is a great pity that Munkhouse, who seems to have been a reasonable surgeon, was such a bad book keeper. By the time of his death at Batavia, he had left no medical records. Only a small portion of his journal remains and it shows him to be an educated and erudite man, his description of New Zealand is one of the best early views of that country and its people.

Surgeon William Brougham Munkhouse, a small pastel portrait by an unknown artist, c.1768.

Wagtails painted by Parkinson. Banks kept the yellow wagtail in a cage in the great cabin where it lived on flies, until one of the ship's cats ate it.

Munkhouse, had been the surgeon aboard *Niger* when Banks had voyaged to Newfoundland in 1766, and must have been delighted to meet him again aboard *Endeavour*. During the voyage they frequently explored islands together, tracking high into the centre of Otaheiti searching for medicinal plants, compiling 'vocabularies', that were the earliest language dictionaries from the Society Islands, New Zealand and New Holland, and discussing astronomy, flora and fauna at dinner around the great cabin table. Only one cloud appeared in their friendship and this was a quarrel over a 'very pretty girl with a fire in her eyes' on Otaheiti, but this appears to have soon been forgotten.

The health of everyone on *Endeavour* appears to have been generally good for the first two years. There were probably the common complaints of ruptures, strains, ulcers and rheumatics, and various journals list three outbreaks of scurvy, which were successfully treated with the 'rob of oranges and lemons', and a number of bilious complaints of varying duration.

Shortly after their arrival in Otaheiti Cook reported 24 seamen and nine marines infected with venereal disease:

> the Women were so very liberal with their favours, or else Nails, Shirts and etc were temptations that they could not withstand, that this distemper very soon spread it self over the greatest part of the Ships Compney but now I have the satisfaction to find that the Natives all agree that we did not bring it here. However this is little satisfaction to them who must suffer by it in a very great degree and may in time spread it self over all the Islands in the South Seas, to the eternal reproach of those who first brought it among them. I had taken the greatest pains to discover if any of the Ships Company had the disorder upon him for above a month before our arrival here and ordered the Surgeon to examine every man the least suspected who declar'd to me that only one man in the Ship was the least affected with it and his complaint was a carious shin bone; this man has not had connection with one woman in the Island.

It is not certain what they were suffering from, as yaws, which looks similar to syphilis, was common amongst the natives, and although not a venereal disease it responded to the same treatment of arsenical injection.

Of the 94 who set out from England in August 1768, eight had died by October 1770 — Alexander Weir, the quartermaster, and Peter Flower, able seaman, were accidently drowned; Forby Sutherland, able seaman, died of consumption and was buried at Botany Bay; boatswain's mate John Reading died from an excess of rum; marine private William Greenslade committed suicide by jumping overboard after being accused of theft and socially ostracised by his fellow marines, and Banks had lost three of his group, Alexander Buchan the artist died in Otaheiti from epilepsy, and his two black servants Thomas Richmond and George Dorton, of hypothermia, in Tierra del Fuego. Eight deaths, but not one from disease caught on the voyage, a remarkable record for the period — unfortunately not one that was to last.

After leaving Australia Cook put into the island of Savu, where he entertained the Rajah to dinner, and took on fresh supplies. Then he set sail for the Dutch colony of Batavia on Java, where he would be able to see the extent of the damage caused on the reef, and to undertake proper repairs. *Endeavour* dropped anchor in the port of Batavia, on 9 October 1770, and within a few days the first cases of fever (malaria) were reported. Surgeon Munkhouse was the first to die on 5 November, followed by the two natives from Otaheiti, Tupia and Tarheto who were returning to England with Banks; then able seamen Timothy Rearden and John Woodworth. Everybody, apart from the sailmaker, was ill with fevers and stomach disorders.

William Perry was promoted to surgeon and set up tents ashore for the sick, and Banks rented a house away from the town for himself and Dr Solander who was very ill. Cook sent his own servant to look after them, but Banks sent him back to the ship as Cook himself went down with malaria. Repairs were held up and it was late December before they were completed. Cook signed on 19 extra seamen and sailed for the Cape of Good Hope, on 26 December 1770. Forty of his original crew were on the sick list, and the rest were still recovering. Shortly after sailing the bloody flux (dysentery) struck, and in the confines of the small ship, it quickly spread. By the end of January, only four men could be mustered for each watch, and twenty three men died on the eleven week voyage to the Cape.

Those who died included Herman Sporing and the artist Sydney Parkinson, from Banks's party; Charles Green, the astronomer and his servant John Reynolds; midshipman Jonathan Munkhouse, the surgeon's younger brother; John Satterley, the carpenter, and two of his crew; John Truslove, the corporal of marines and private Daniel Preston; the cook John Thompson, and John Ravenhill, the sailmaker. The effect of seeing so many shipmates dying — in one week eleven were buried at sea — can barely be imagined. Two or three seamen who were not ill, but thought they recognised symptoms, suffered a form of hysteria and needed to be restrained. The journals at this time reflect the sadness and melancholia on board, recording only the very basic daily shipboard activities and the continuing deaths. It is fair to say that the life had gone out of the ship.

When *Endeavour* reached the Cape on 14 March 1771, the disease had peaked and done its worst, although the master, Richard Molyneux and lieutenant Zachary Hicks were still very ill, and Dr Solander was confined to his bed. He got up two weeks later 'for the first time, very much emaciated by his tedious illness'.

Burial at sea.

Tents were again set on shore for the sick and William Perry ordered new medicines and foods for his patients. Shore leave was granted, and Banks and his servants went foraging for s-pecimens, while lieutenant John Gore felt well enough to climb Table Mountain. With ten more men signed on, *Endeavour* left harbour on 14 April and set sail for St Helena island. Three days later the master Robert Molyneux died and was buried at sea. They dropped anchor at St Helena two weeks later, and after a short stay to overhaul and replenish stores, Cook sailed in company with a convoy of merchant East Indiamen for England. On 10 May Lieutenant Zachary Hicks was very ill and a doctor from one of the East Indiamen rowed over to attend him, but could not help. He died two weeks later 'of a Consumption which he was not free from when we saild from England so that it may be truly said that he hath been dieing every since' wrote Cook.

Banks continued to take his boat out when possible, but found little new to report, apart from the death of his spaniel:

My Bitch Lady was found dead in my Cabbin laying upon a stool on which she generaly slept. She had been re-markably well for some days; in the night she shreikd out so very loud so that we who slept in the great Cabbin heard her, but becoming quiet immediately no one regarded it.

Six days later Nick Young was at the masthead at noon when he sighted Lands End. It was 11 July 1771, and *Endeavour* had come home.

Endings

"I have however made no great discoveries"

W hen *Endeavour* was safely moored in the Downs on 12 July, Cook wrote to the Admiralty Secretary announcing the ship's arrival and his intention to come immediately to the Admiralty Office with all the ship's journals, logs, charts and various 'curiosity's' (artefacts from the voyage). He reported also the state and condition of His Majesty's Bark *Endeavour*:

> *Complement 85, Borne 82, Musterd 80, Widows' Men 2, Sick 19, Supernumerarys 8. Provisions on board: 21 days bread, 28 days arrack, 4 days beef, 4 days pork, 4 weeks pease, oatmeal or rice, 4 weeks sugar: water 10 tons. Condition of the Bark: Foul.*

Cook soon received his rewards: he was promoted to the rank of Commander and highly commended. On 14 August 1771 the King received him at St James Palace, and three days later Cook wrote to his old mentor John Walker at Whitby 'I had the honour of a hours Conference with the King the other day who was pleased to express his Approbation of my Conduct in Terms that were extremely pleasing to me...'

Cook had other letters to write, letters of condolence to the families of his men who had died, and letters of recommendation. As soon as he could, he hurried back to Elizabeth at 7 Assembly Row, to find James and Nathaniel well and grown. Sadly his daugher Elizabeth had died at the age of four, just three months before his return, and Joseph, born after he had set sail in 1768,

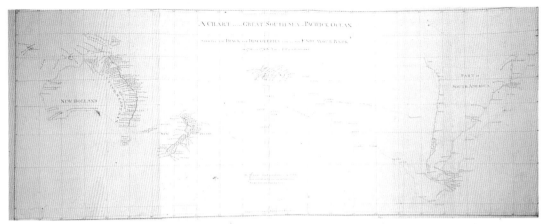

A CHART .... GREAT SOUTH SEA ... PACIFICK OCEAN

.... TRACK ... DISCOVERIES .... ENDEAVOUR BARK

NEW HOLLAND

PART of SOUTH AMERICA

Chart of the Great South Sea and Pacific Ocean, drawn aboard Endeavour *by James Cook and Issac Smith.*

Watercolour painting by Parkinson of one of the new plants found in New Holland (Australia) and named Banksia, after Joseph Banks.

had lived only a few months. Elizabeth and the boys were overjoyed to see him back safe and well, and he spent many hours telling them of his adventures and the places and people he had visited. He brought them gifts, and perhaps he gave them the ship's goat as a pet, for she went somewhere on the Mile End Road. Hopefully she found the just reward as penned for her by Dr Samuel Johnson:

In fame scarce second to the nurse of Jove
This Goat, who twice the world had traversed round,
Deserving both her master's care and love,
Ease and perpetual pasture now has found.

Joseph Banks and Dr Solander had completed the most successful British scientific expedition yet undertaken in the South Pacific, collecting more than 30,000 plants, which yielded over 3,600 known species and over 1,400 new ones, as well as 1,000 species of animals; the whole collection was supported by some 1,240 drawings and paintings. They had also brought back a representative collection of art and artefacts of the South Seas, and compiled the first language dictionaries of that area. Back in London, Banks and Solander were feted by society and scientific circles. Banks was presented to King George III at St James Palace, and both he and Dr Solander were invited to confer further with His Majesty at Richmond.

The officers and men now went their own ways, some home to their families and friends, some to new ships, and some to rejoin Cook on his second and third voyages, It is sure that wherever they went, they talked for many months about what they had seen and the dangers they had encountered during their circumnavigation of the world. Of his officers and men Cook said, 'they have gone through the Fatigues and dangers of the whole Voyage with that cheerfulness and Allertness that will always do Honour to British Seamen'.

Of the voyage Cook wrote:

I however have made no very great Discoveries yet I have exploard more of the Great South Sea than any that have gone before me so much that little remains now to be done to have a thorough knowledge of that part of the Globe. I sayled from England as well provided For such a voyage as possible and a better ship For such a Service I never would wish for.

Cook had fulfilled his orders from the Royal Society and the Admiralty. The transit of Venus had been successfully observed by three separate parties on Otaheiti, and he had surveyed and charted that island. He had explored more of the South Seas than anyone previously, and had touched on forty previously undiscovered islands. Following his secret orders he had sailed westward in the hope of discovering *Terra Australis Incognita*, but had found the land known as New Zeland (New Zealand), which he circumnavigated, surveyed and charted in great detail. Continuing westwards the *Endeavour* reached New South Wales (the eastern part of Australia) and sailed northward, observing, surveying and charting, and finally rounded the northern tip, to verify the existence of a strait between that country and New Guinea. During the voyage, with the assistance of the latest navigational equipment and knowledge, Cook had been able to calculate longitude at sea, with great accuracy.

The first chart of New Zealand compiled by Cook and Smith, after circumnavigating and charting both islands from October 1769 to April 1770.

The voyage of the *Endeavour* had been full of adventure — exotic lands and people, unknown plants, birds and animals, an exciting brush with death on the Great Barrier Reef, and the tragedy of so many dead after Batavia — all these ingredients captured the imagination of the British public, and set James Cook's path for life. Rather less romantically, the King and the Government could see possible new colonies and economic advantages for Britain, and, eager to beat the French to the prizes, within a few months they found money and two new ships to send James Cook on his second expedition 1772-75.

James Cook would spend the remainder of his life exploring and surveying the Pacific Ocean, from Antarctica to Alaska. His skills as a seaman, his thirst for knowledge and adventure, together with his courage, humanity and determination, had enabled him to rise from humble beginnings to captain in the Royal Navy, and he is justly remembered as one of the greatest British explorers and navigators of all time.

The Ship's Crew List

The list is taken from Beaglehole (see p.85) which he compiled from the *Endeavour's* muster books, but does not include the men taken on at Batavia and the Cape.

Order: name, place of birth, age, rank and biographical details

ANDERSON Robert, Inverness, 28, AB: gunner *Resolution* 2nd & 3rd voyage.
BOOTIE John, midshipman, died dysentery 4.2.1771.
CHARLTON John, London, 15, captain's servant 1.5.1770: Cook's servant *Greville* 1765-8.
CHILDS Joseph, Dublin, 29, AB & Ship's cook from 1.2.1771.
CLERKE Charles, Essex, 25, master's mate & 3rd lieutenant 26.5.1771: 2nd ltn *Resolution* 2nd voyage, commander *Discovery* 3rd voyage, died before returning to England 1779.
COLLETT William, Buckinghamshire, 20, AB: AB *Resolution* 2nd voyage.
COOK James, Yorkshire, 40, 1st lieutenant.
COX Matthew, Dorset, 22, AB: punished stealing Maori potatoes Bay of Islands.
DAWSON William, Deptford, 19, AB: AB *Resolution* 2nd voyage.
DOZEY John, the Brazils, 20, AB, died at the Cape 7.4.1771.
EVANS Samuel, Quartermaster & boatswain 5.2.1771.
FLOWER Peter, Guernsey, 18, AB, drowned at Rio de Janeiro 2.12.1768: had served with Cook five years.
FORWOOD Stephen, gunner, ringleader stealing rum 2.12.1769.
GATHREY John, boatswain, died dysentery 4.2.1771.
GOODJOHN John, AB: In 1791 he petitioned Banks for help, Banks gave him a guinea.
GORE John, 3rd lieutenant & 2nd lieutenant on Hicks death: went with Banks to Iceland 1772, 1st lieutenant *Resolution* 3rd voyage and after Clerke's death took command, Captain Greenwich Hospital.
GRAY James, Leith, 24, AB: & quartermaster 5.2.1771: boatswain *Resolution* 2nd voyage.
HAITE Francis, Kent, 42, carpenter's crew, died 30.1.1771
HARDMAN Thomas, London, 33, boatswain's mate & AB & sailmaker.
HARVEY William, London, 17, Hick's servant, & AB & Midshipman 7.2.1771: midshipman *Resolution* 2nd voyage, masters mate *Resolution* 3rd voyage.
HICKS Zachary, Stepney, 29, 2nd lieutenant, died 26 May 1771 of consumption.
HOWSON William, London, 16, Captain's servant
HUGHES Richard, London, 22, carpenters mate & carpenter 15.8.1771.
HUTCHINS Richard, Deptford, 27, boatswain's mate & boatswain, punished 16.4.1769 for disobedience.

JEFFS Henry, ship's butcher, punished for assault on Tahitian woman, died 27.2.1771.
JOHNSON Isaac, Cheshire, 26, AB.
JONES Samuel, London, 22, AB: Applied to Banks for help January 1786.
JONES Thomas (1st), surgeon Munkhouse's servant: His widow petitioned Banks for help 1791.
JONES Thomas (2nd), Wales, 27, AB.
JORDAN Benjamin, Deptford, 30, AB, died 31.1.1771
JORDAN Thomas, boatswain's servant, deserted in the river Thames 12 Septermber 1771.
KNIGHT Thomas, AB.
LITTLEBOY Michael, Deptford, 20, AB: petitioned Banks 1787 for help in obtaining a Custom House berth.
LITTLEBOY Richard, Deptford, 25, AB, punished stealing rum 2.12.1769.
MAGRA James Maria, New York, AB & midshipman 27.5.1771: author of a plan for colonising New South Wales, British consul at Teneriffe, secretary to British embassy at Constantinople, consul at Tangier.
MATTHEWS Thomas, servant to ship's cook.
MOLYNEUX Robert, Lancashire, 22, master, died 17.4.1771.
MUNKHOUSE Jonathan, midshipman, brother to surgeon, died 6.2.1771.
MUNKHOUSE William Brougham, surgeon, died Batavia of fever 5.11.1770.
MOODY Samuel, Worcester, 40, AB, carpenters crew, died 30.1.1771
MOREY Nathaniel, lieutenant Gore's servant.
NICHOLSON James, Scotland, 21, AB, punished theft Otaheiti, died 31.1.1771.
NOWELL George, AB carpenter's crew & carpenter 12.2.1771.
ORTON Richard, captain's clerk, had his ears cut during a drunken joke.
PARKER Isaac, Ipswich, 27, AB & boatswains mate 25.3.1769.
PECKOVER William, Northamptonshire, 21, AB: gunner *Discovery* 3rd voyage: After voyage requested recommendation for a job from Banks.
PEREIRA Manoel, entered at Rio 2.12.1768, AB, punished for stealing Maori potatoes, died 27.2.1771.
PERRY William, Chiswick, 21, surgeon's mate & surgeon on death of Munkhouse.
PICKERSGILL Richard, Yorkshire, 19, master's mate & master on Moyneux's death: 3rd Lieutenant *Resolution* 2nd voyage: slipped and drowned in river Thames July 1779.

PONTO Antonio, Venice, 24, AB.
RAMSAY John, Plymouth, 21, AB: ship's cooks
Resolution 2nd voyage and AB 3rd voyage, became a
pensioner of the Chelsea Chest.
RAVENHILL John Hull, 49, sailmaker. Cook said he
was old man about 70 or 80, and drunk every day,
died 27.1.1771.
READING John, Kinsale, 24, boatswain's mate,
punished at Rio for not punishing others correctly,
died at sea excess of rum 28.8.1769.
REARDEN Timothy, Ireland, 25, AB, died Batavia
24.12.1770.
ROBERTS Daniel, gunner's servant, died 2.2.1771.
SATTERLEY John, carpenter, died 12.1.1771: Cook said 'a
Man such Esteem'd by me and every Gentleman on board'.
SAUNDERS Patrick, midshipman, disated AB
23.5.1770, deserted Batavia 25.12.1770
SIMMONDS Thomas, Brentford Middlesex, 24, AB.
SIMPSON Alexander, AB, punished stealing rum
2.12.1769, died 21.1.1771.
SMITH Isaac, London, 16, AB, midshipman & masters
mate. First to land at Botany Bay, assisted Cook in
surveying: masters mate *Resolution* 2nd voyage. Became
post-captain 1787, superannuated Rear Admiral 1807.
Was Mrs Cook's cousin and lived with her for many years.
STAINSBY Robert, Darlington, 27, AB.
STEPHENS Henry, Falmouth, 28, AB, punished for
refusing to eat fresh beef and for stealing potatoes in
New Zealand.
SUTHERLAND Forby, Orkneys, 29, AB, died at
Botany Bay 1.5.1770 of consumption.
TAYLOR Robert, armourer.
THOMPSON John, one handed ship's cook, died
31.1.1771.
THURMAN John, 20, AB impressed for New York
sloop at Funchal 14.9.1768.
TUNLEY James, Blackwall London, 24, AB.
WEIR Alexander, Scotland, 35, quartermaster,
drowned off Funchal 14.9.1768.
WILKINSON Francis, Wales, AB, master's mate, died
August 1771.
WILLIAMS Charles, Bristol, 38, AB.
WOLFE Archibald, Scotland, 38, AB, punished
Otaheiti stealing nails, died 31.1.1771.
WOODWORTH John, AB, died Batavia 24.12.1770.

MARINES
EDGCUMBE John, sergeant: lieutenant of marines
Resolution 2nd voyage.
BOWLES John, private.
DUNSTER Thomas, private, punished refusing
allowance of fresh beef 16.9.1768, died 25.1.1771.

GIBSON Samuel, private, deserted at Otaheiti
9.7.1769: corporal of Marines *Resolution* 2nd voyage,
sergeant *Resolution* 3rd voyage.
GREENSLAND William, private, commited suicide
overboard 26.3.1769.
JUDGE William, private, punished for abusive language
to officer of the watch 30.11.1769.
PAUL Henry, private.
PRESTON Daniel, private, died 15.2.1771.
ROSSITER Thomas, drummer, punished for stealing rum
2.12.1769, and for drunkenness and assualt 21.2.177.
TRUSLOVE John, corporal, died 24.1.1771.
WILSHIRE William, private: wrote to Banks for help
23.8.1802 who gave him a guinea.
WEBB Clement, private, deserted Otaheiti 9.7.1769:
wrote to Banks 1808 crippled by an accident and
needed a pension.

SUPERNUMERARIES
GREEN Charles, 33, astronomer, died from dysentery
29.1.1771.
REYNOLD John, Green's servant, died from dysentery
18.12.1770.
BANKS Joseph, 24, botanist and Fellow of the Royal Society:
Endeavour's voyage made him famous, became president of
Royal Society 1778 to his death, adviser to George III and a
great patron of the natural sciences, died 1820.
SOLANDER Daniel Carl, 35, Sweden, naturalist:
Banks's librarian 1771-82, Keeper Natural history
Department at Bristish Musuem 1773. Died 17 May
1782 of a massive cerebral haemorrhage, at Banks's
house in Soho. Banks acted as his pallbearer.
PARKINSON Sydney, 23, artist, Scotland, died 26
January 1771 of dysentry, on voyage to the Cape.
BUCHAN Alexander, artist, died at Otaheiti, 17 April
1769 of epilepsy and was buried at sea.
SPORING Herman Deidrich, Sweden, secretary and
assistant, died 25 January 1771 of dysentry, on the
voyage to the Cape.
ROBERTS James, aged 16, Lincolnshire, Banks's servant
and assistant.
BRISCOE Peter, Banks's servant and assistant since his
Oxford days.
RICHMOND Thomas, Banks's Black servant, died of
hypothermia January 1769.
DALTON George, Banks's Black servant, died of
hypothermia January 1769.
YOUNG Nick, boy, taken on 18.4.69 inlieu of Buchan.
with Banks to Iceland.
TUPIA, Native of Otaheiti, died Batavia 20.12.1770.
TARHETO, his servant, died Batavia 17.12.1770.

Acknowledgements

I, like anyone who attempts to write about the voyage of HM Bark *Endeavour*, Lieutenant James Cook and his crew, owe a huge debt of gratitude to the late Dr JC Beaglehole, who thoroughly and eruditely covered the bulk of the available source material, and produced four volumes on his findings, which will never be bettered.

I would also like to thank Harold B Carter for his definitive work on Sir Joseph Banks, and for his time, comments and assistance, so freely given. Brian Lavery of National Maritime Museum, Greenwich, for his knowledge, readily shared, and comments on the text. And thanks to all the helpful staff, too many to name individually, at the National Maritime Museum, Greenwich, the British Library, the National Art Library, London, the Public Record Office, Kew, the Natural History Museum, London. Bruce Stannard, and John Longley, Chief Executive Officer of Endeavour Foundation for their comments on the text, and to Arthur Weller Chairman of the Endeavour Foundation for his constant encouragement.

Antonia Macarthur

Sources for Photographs and Illustrations

2/3   The Mitchell Library, State Library of NSW
5   National Maritime Museum, Greenwich, BHR4227
6   By kind permission of the Whitby Museum, Whitby, North Yorkshire, England
7   The Mitchell Library, the State Library of NSW From *Whitby To Wapping* by Julia Hunt
8   By kind permission of the Guildhall Library, Corporation of London
13   By kind permission of Jack Frost
14   National Maritime Museum, Greenwich, D3356
15   Tooley Collection, National Library of Australia, Map T1002
16   By kind permission of John Longley
20   British Library, Add 23920 f8
      By kind permission of Natural History Museum, London, TO7474/r
21   National Maritime Museum, Greenwich, D7008
22   Maritime Heritage Press
24/25 Inset: British Library, Add 9345 6V; Photo: Andrew Halsall
26   British Library, Add 9345 f57
27   National Maritime Museum, Greenwich, DR3819
29   Photo: Rod Mcleod
31   Photo: Ross Shardlow
32   British Library, MS7085 f39
34   National Maritime Museum, Greenwich, DR3817
35   By kind permission of the Natural History Museum, London, TO9195/r
38   Photo: Robert Garvey
39   Photo: John Lancaster
42   Author's photograph
43   Author's photograph

45   British Library, Add 7085 f8ii
46   British Library, Add 7085 f8iv
47   National Maritime Museum, Greenwich, B3134
48   By kind permission of the Linnaean Society of London
49   By kind permission of the Natural History Museum, London, TO4264/r
      By kind permission of the Natural History Museum, London, TO9217/r
50   British Library, Add 23920 f14A
51   By kind permission of the Lincolnshire County Council: Usher Gallery, Lincoln
54   By kind permission of the National Library of Australia, 3680
55   By kind permission of Government House, Wellington, New Zealand
57   British Library, Add 23920 f44
61   The Mitchell Library, the State Library of NSW
62   Photo: Rod Mcleod
63   British Library, Add 23921 f6a
64   By kind permission of Natural History Museum, London, TO5390/4
67   Photo: Rod Mcleod
      Author's photograph
69   Australian Naval Photographic Unit
73   British Library, Add 7085 f21
74   By courtesy of Christie's Images, London
      By kind permission of the Natural History Museum, London
80   British Library, Add 7085 f1
      By kind permission of Natural History Museum, London, TO7326/r
81   British Library, Add 7085 f17

Primary Sources

Public Records Office, London

ADM95/17: Admiralty Orders

ADM95/94: Deptford Yard Books 1768

ADM106/1163: Letters Cook to Navy Board 1768-72

ADM106/2508: Standing Orders to Yards from Navy Board 1756-82

ADM51/4546: *Endeavour* journal of 1st Lieutenant Zachary Hicks

ADM51/4548: *Endeavour* journal of 2nd Lieutenant John Gore

ADM51/4546: *Endeavour* journal of Master Richard Molyneux

ADM51/4547: *Endeavour* journal of Master's mate Richard Pickersgill

ADM51/4548: *Endeavour* journal of Master's mate Charles Clerke

ADM51/4547: *Endeavour* journal of Master's mate Francis Wilkinson

ADM51/4545: *Endeavour* journal of Gunner Stephen Forwood

ADM51/4546: *Endeavour* journal of Midshipman John Bootie

ADM51/4545: *Endeavour* journal of Astronomer Charles Green; also Barbados trip 1763

National Maritime Museum, Greenwich

ADM168/144: Specifications for 32 gun Frigate, 1760

British Library

ADD27889: Portion of *Endeavour* journal of Surgeon W.B. Munkhouse

Banks Archive Project, Natural History Museum

Volunteers Volume letters and accounts

Selected Bibliography

Beaglehole, JC ed. *The Journals of Captain James Cook on His Voyage of Discovery. The Voyage of the Endeavour 1768-1771 Vol 1*, Cambridge 1955
The Endeavour Journal of Joseph Banks Vol I & II, Sydney, 1962
The Life of Captain James Cook Adam & Charles Black, London, 1974

Carter, HB *Sir Joseph Banks* British Museum (Natural History), 1988

Chapman, Fredrick af *Architectura Navalis Mercatoria* Stockholm, 1768

Harland, James *Seamanship in the Age of Sail* London, 1984

Henning, Henningsen *Crossing the Equator* Copenhagen, 1961

Lavery, Brian *The Arming and Fitting of English Ships of War 1600-1815*, 1987

Lewis, Michael *A Social History of the Navy*, 1960

MacGregor, David R *Merchant Sailing Ships, Sovereignty of Sail 1775-1815*, 1985

Porter, Roy *English Society in the Eighteenth Century*, 1982

Rochefoucauld, Jean Marchand, ed. *A Frenchman in England, 1784* Cambridge, 1933

Rodger, NAM *The Wooden World An Anatomy of the Georgian Navy*, 1986

Singer, Charles & Underwood, E A *A Short History of Medicine*, 1962

Sutherland, William *Britain's Glory, or Shipbuilding Unveil'd*, 172